"A well-written, accessible text suitable for advanced undergraduate and graduate students. The authors build a solid foundation in the economics of media as it has mainly been developed in western countries, and apply it with excellent effect to understand Indian television, newspapers, film and other media."

David Waterman, *Professor Emeritus of The Media School, Indiana University*

"The academic study of the media and its management in India has not kept pace with the transformation of the media industry, which has grown exponentially in the past two decades. Elavarthi and Chitrapu's timely book fills an existing gap in scholarship in this field and would be extremely useful for students and researchers."

Daya K. Thussu, *Professor of International Communication, Hong Kong Baptist University*

"The authors have written a must-read primer for anyone considering a career in media economics and management. It is a valuable resource for all students, teachers, scholars, and practitioners in the media industries."

Sundeep R. Muppidi, *Professor of Communication, University of Hartford*

"Two excellent scholars have provided a highly readable and comprehensive introduction to an important field of study. This book will be a superb guide for students and scholars interested in understanding the economic forces and factors that shape the workings of media industries and institutions."

Aswin Punathambekar, *Professor of Media Studies, University of Virginia*

MEDIA ECONOMICS AND MANAGEMENT

This book offers a comprehensive understanding of key concepts and terms in media economics and management and explains their applications using relevant data. Beginning with a conceptual study of media markets, industry structures, firm behaviour, public policy, production, pricing and consumption choices in media industries, the book uses the framework to present an in-depth examination of the management of four major media industry sectors in India: newspaper publishing, television broadcasting, film and digital media industries. It also deals with two topics relevant across media business sectors: creative industries approaches and copyright issues. The book discusses the economic forces and factors that shape the workings of media industries and institutions in India to highlight trends in a business that is rapidly evolving, highly profitable and marked by regional, linguistic, economic and cultural diversity. This volume is a step towards formalising the emerging field of media economics and management within the discipline of mass communication and journalism as an area of research and education in India.

An accessible guide to the basic principles and concepts of media economics and management, with illustrations from Indian and global media industries, this will be an essential resource for students, researchers and teachers of media and communication studies, media economics and management, political economy and sociology as well as for professionals in media industries.

Sathya Prakash Elavarthi is Associate Professor at the Department of Communication, University of Hyderabad, India. He teaches media management, documentary theory and film theory and criticism. His research interests include political economy of media, media histories, film studies and digital cultures. His recent works include book chapters in *Handbooks in Communication Science: Management and Economics of Communication* (2020), and *Indian Media Economy Vol. II—Market Dynamics and Social Transactions* (2017).

Sunitha Chitrapu is an independent researcher based in Mumbai, India. She is a member of the Advisory Board of the School of Media and Cultural Studies, Tata Institute of Social Sciences, Mumbai, India. She was formerly Head of the Social Communications Media Department, Sophia Polytechnic, Mumbai, where she is currently visiting faculty for Communications Research, Media and Society. Her research interests include the political economy of media, media trade and modernities. Her work has been published in *Culture Unbound, Journal of Creative Communications, Social Movement Studies Journal of Social, Cultural and Political Protest, Handbooks in Communication Science: Management and Economics of Communication* (2020), and in *Indian Media Economy Vol. II—Market Dynamics and Social Transactions* (2017).

MEDIA ECONOMICS AND MANAGEMENT

Sathya Prakash Elavarthi and Sunitha Chitrapu

Routledge
Taylor & Francis Group

LONDON AND NEW YORK

First published 2022
by Routledge
2 Park Square, Milton Park, Abingdon, Oxon OX14 4RN

and by Routledge
605 Third Avenue, New York, NY 10158

Routledge is an imprint of the Taylor & Francis Group, an informa business

British Library Cataloguing-in-Publication Data
A catalogue record for this book is available from the British Library

Library of Congress Cataloging-in-Publication Data
A catalog record for this book has been requested

ISBN: 978-1-138-50596-4 (hbk)
ISBN: 978-1-032-05799-6 (pbk)
ISBN: 978-1-003-19921-2 (ebk)

DOI: 10.4324/9781003199212

Typeset in Bembo
by Apex CoVantage, LLC

For my mother Sundaramma, who believed in our future despite crushing circumstances.
—*Sathya Prakash Elavarthi*

For Ashwyn, for all his support.
—*Sunitha Chitrapu*

CONTENTS

TABLES

ABBREVIATIONS

AAAI—Advertising Agencies Association of India
ABC—Audit Bureau of Circulations
ABP— *Ananda Bazar Patrika*
APP—Average Physical Product
B2B—Business to Business
BARC—Broadcast Audience Research Council of India
CAGR—Compound Annual Growth Rate
CCI—Competition Commission of India
CPA—cost per acquisition
CPC—cost per click
CPM—cost per thousand impressions
CPT—cost per thousand
CRP—cost per rating point
DAVP—Department of Audio-Visual Publicity
DB— *Dainik Bhaskar*
DIPR—Directorate of Information and Public Relations
DRM—digital rights management
DTH—direct-to-home
DTP—desktop publishing
GDP—Gross Domestic Product
GEC—General Entertainment Channel
GNP—Gross National Product
GNU—General Public licence
GRP—Gross Rating Points
GST—Goods and Service Tax
GUI—graphical user interface
HT— *Hindustan Times*

IFPI—International Federation of the Phonographic Industry
IMI—Indian Music Industry
INR—Indian Rupee
INS—Indian Newspaper Society
INTAM—Indian National Television Audience Measurement
IO—industrial organisation
IPG—interactive programming guide
IPI—Indian Phonographic Industry
IPR—Intellectual Property Rights
IPRS—Indian Performing Rights Society
IPTV—Internet Protocol Television
IRRO—Indian Reprographic Rights Organisation
IRS—Indian Readership Survey
MCN—multi-channel network
MPP—Marginal Physical Product
MRUC—Media Research Users Council
NRS—National Readership Survey
OA—Open Access
OE—organisational ecology
ORG—Operations Research Group
OTT—over the top
PPL—Phonographic Performance Limited
PRC—Principle of Relative Constancy
RERA—Real Estate Regulatory Authority
RNI—Registrar of Newspapers of India
RBV—resources-based view
ROC—Registrar of Companies
RSCI—Research Studies Council of India
SCP—Structure–Conduct–Performance
SVOD—Subscription Video on Demand
TAM—Television Audience Measurement
TOI— *The Times of India*
TRIPS—Trade Related Aspects of Intellectual Property Rights
TRP—Television Rating Points
TVOD—Transactional Video on Demand
TVR—Television Ratings
VOD—Video on Demand
VR—Virtual Reality
WIPO—World Intellectual Property Organisation
WTO—World Trade Organisation

FOREWORD

The economics of the media has received far less scholarly attention in India compared to pursuits by peers elsewhere and, perhaps more importantly, what its media landscape deserves. Despite three decades of the so-called media boom in India, the insufficiency of a social science engagement with the economics of this boom, and that of its recent erosion, remains somewhat of a mystery.

Although the last decade has witnessed periodic and increasing press reportage and public discussion in the press over the media business, these oscillate between two extremes: either glowing accounts of activities of select media companies, including their expansion and stock valuations, or concerns over the viability and sustainability of certain businesses, especially in the news media. Both these articulations are short of a systematic and conceptually informed understanding of the economics of the media industries in India. This has been ascribed equally to the muted development of media studies as an academic field of inquiry in India and its sub-field, media economics, being marginalised therein (Parthasarathi et al. 2020). More surprising is mainstream economics and management studies in India, known to take up frontier areas, also being tentative in exploring this exciting sub-field of media studies.

While media economics offers a macro perspective of the political economy of the media, the meso and micro perspectives are often pursued under the scholarly rubric of media management as well (see von Rimscha 2020). This book marks an important contribution in relating key concepts in this sub-field of media studies with knowledge about media businesses in India that will be of use in both these areas—political economy of the media as well as media management. It speaks to the needs of the increasing number of university departments, variedly dealing with media studies, mass communication and journalism, offering courses in media economics, media management and, more generally, the political economy of the Indian media. For students in these programmes, both at the undergraduate and research levels, this work by Sathya Prakash Elavarthi and Sunitha Chitrapu offers a handy and much-needed reference point to all such teaching/learning initiatives.

Whether the workings of newspapers, television and cinema in India indicate a modern industrial activity or is akin to other businesses organised along traditional, familial lines is itself a matter of debate. In either case, however, understanding their economic organisation and dynamics becomes the key, including if we choose to wade into such a debate. This book seeks to reach out to a multiplicity of constituencies, including those who do not primarily identify themselves as students of economics. Pioneers in the discipline of media economics have identified four methodological approaches in this field, namely trend studies, financial analysis, econometrics, and case studies (Albarran 2005). Of these, financial analysis and case studies have evinced most interest in books from India, Kohli's work (Kohli Khandekar 2013) being a long-standing illustration of the attempt to blend these two approaches. In venturing beyond these methodological thrusts, important as they are, we would also be able to better appreciate the heterodoxies increasingly marking the approaches and analytical emphases in media economics (see Fitzgerald and Winseck 2018).

In an era where the media occupies a pivotal role in society and politics, the study of its economics is too consequential a matter to be left to professional economists alone. This, then, also demands the teaching of the economics of the media in India be obliged to reach out to students from a wide array of disciplines or motivated by varied professional concerns. Unpacking the economics of the media is therefore also very much part of the larger pursuit of media literacy. Immersed in this sensibility, this book takes up the challenge to further such pursuits. By linking basic concepts and theoretical formulations about key media sectors with the experiences of what we see about their performance and behaviour, the authors speak to this need. No doubt, the media tend to perform in ways similar to many other economic activities. While explicating this, the authors also try to clarify how the media are different from other economic activities and why its characteristics may inform different types of decision making.

In other words, Elavarthi and Chitrapu have addressed what is known about the economics of the media in India as also what calls for being explored more granularly. In this sense, the book is part of an ongoing intellectual churn in media studies in India striving to conceptualise not only processes of economic change intrinsic to the workings of the media, but also the role of extra-economic logics in shaping these processes. This is but one way in which the book contributes to inculcating a critical media literacy amongst its readers, be they inclined towards traditions of political economy or management, or those with professional or wider academic interests.

Vibodh Parthasarathi
Jamia Millia Islamia, New Delhi, India

References

Albarran, A. B. (2005). Media economics research: Methodological perspectives and areas for future development. *Palabra Clave 13, 8*(2), 115–124. Retrieved March 20, 2021, from https://palabraclave.unisabana.edu.co/index.php/palabraclave/article/view/1463/1631

Fitzgerald, S., and Winseck, D. R. (2018, July). Media economics: Missed opportunities, mischaracterizations. *The Political Economy of Communication* [S.l.], *6*(1). Retrieved March 20, 2021, from www.polecom.org/index.php/polecom/article/view/92

Kohli-Khandekar, V. (2013). *The Indian Media Business* (Fourth Ed.). Thousand Oaks, CA: Sage Publications.

Parthasarathi, V., Chitrapu, S., and Elavarthi, S. P. (2020). Media economics in India: Traversing the Rubicon? In M. Bjørn Rimscha (Ed.), *Handbooks of Communication Science: Management and Economics of Communication*. Boston/Berlin: De Gruyter Mouton.

von Rimscha, M. B. (2020). Management and economics of media and communication: History and definition of the field. In M. Bjørn von Rimscha (Ed.), *Handbooks of Communication Science: Management and Economics of Communication*. Boston/Berlin: De Gruyter Mouton.

PREFACE

At the beginning of the second decade of the 21st century, we find that Indian media industries are diverse, rapidly evolving and highly profitable, attracting media and business students seeking professional careers in them. While we have well-established traditions of media research from critical and policy perspectives that have examined the Indian media as social, political and cultural entities, the economic aspect is still in a nascent stage in the areas of mass communications and their intersections with social sciences and humanities, despite its continued presence in many graduate and undergraduate course curricula across the country (the bachelor's degree programme in journalism started by Hislop College affiliated to Nagpur University in 1964 was one the earliest to have a full paper on newspaper business management). These undergraduate and post-graduate programmes have relied on the several excellent textbooks on media economics that are available internationally, and current curricula on media economics and management in communication departments cover many more industries besides print by including research journal articles, industry reports and a few other publications. This book builds on all these efforts and also supplements them in many ways.

While the economics of media are universal, Indian media industries demand more research attention than they have received this far. Linguistic, economic and cultural diversity in India make it a country of not one but several media industries and markets, and this diversity is important to understand if we want to explore the economics of Indian media industries. While there are some reference books in this area, we hope that this book will fulfil the long-felt need for a textbook on media economics and management that can provide a good grounding in the fundamentals of media economics for post-graduate and undergraduate students. We hope that in addition to serving its role in media education, this book will also play a key role in formalising the new and emerging area of media economics and management as an area of research in India.

Towards that end, this book is organised into ten chapters. The first four chapters present a broad conceptual framework of media markets, industry structures, firm behaviour, advertising markets, public policy, production, pricing and consumption choices in media industries. Beginning with an understanding of media products as public goods and their dual product markets, the first chapter examines demand uncertainty, media market structures, firm behaviour and media industry lifecycles. The second chapter builds on these concepts by examining revenue streams in media industries, cost structures, economies of scale and scope, production functions, demand and pricing in product and advertising markets. The third chapter focuses on audiences and advertising markets including the principle of relative constancy and media audience measurement. The fourth chapter builds on these ideas by presenting a view of media industries and public policy with special reference to market deficiencies, abuse of market dominance and information asymmetries and policy interventions for the same.

Chapters 5 through 8 use the framework presented in the first four chapters to provide an in-depth look into four key media industry sectors in India—newspaper publishing, television broadcasting, film and digital media industries—and their business and regulatory environments. We examine the fundamental role played by language and geography in the Indian media industries. Chapter 5 presents an in-depth look at the newspaper industry, including segmentation, cost reduction and revenue maximisation strategies and the challenges offered by digital media to this sector in India. Chapter 6 deals with the television industry, its market segments, revenue streams, pricing and distribution strategies and key challenges faced by this industry. Chapter 7 examines the film industry, horizontal and vertical integration in its segments and revenue streams, and emerging trends in distribution, financing and exports. Chapter 8 deals with digital media with an emphasis on over-the-top platforms (OTTs) and digital rights management (DRM) issues in this sector.

The last two chapters of the book deal with two topics that are relevant to all sectors of the media business: the creative industries approach, and copyright issues. Chapter 9 offers a view of the context within which media industries operate using the creative industries perspective to discuss risk, innovation and the nature of work in these industries. Chapter 10 addresses copyright terms, issues and debates with appropriate case studies. Given the current scope, we could cover only four industry sectors in this edition: newspaper publishing, television, film and digital media. Future editions may include sectors such as book publishing, radio, music and gaming to make the work even more comprehensive.

We have attempted to provide a wide-ranging analysis of the research literature in the area of media economics and management, taking into consideration international and Indian contexts while presenting examples and data to illustrate key concepts, policy and market analysis, so that they are relevant and accessible to students interested in these topics. We also hope that a broader understanding of the Indian media as economic entities will further inform and strengthen future media research from critical and policy perspectives.

ACKNOWLEDGEMENTS

While the cover carries only the authors' names, this book has been made possible thanks to the support and patience of many. This book is a direct result of our years in the classroom. We would like to thank in particular our students who provide a focus for our efforts. Through their questions and interactions, they have contributed to the creation of learning communities that extend well beyond the classroom. They have motivated our efforts to stay abreast of the developments in the dynamic environments that constitute the Indian media industries.

At the University of Hyderabad's Department of Communication, Prof. Vinod Pavarala and Prof. P. Thirumal played an important role in encouraging this endeavour. The Department of Communication was also generous in providing study leave for the crucial work done at the initial stages of the book. Former students Aditya Deshbandu and Gargi Shivanand were kind enough to give feedback on some draft chapters.

We acknowledge the active encouragement and support received from Prof. Adrian Athique, University of Queensland; Dr. Vibodh Parthasarathi, Centre for Culture, Media and Governance, Jamia Millia Islamia; Prof. S.V. Srinivas, Azim Premji University. We thank Prof. David Waterman, Indiana University, for his comments on our draft.

We would also like to thank our families, who took on additional responsibilities so that we could devote our attention to the book. Sathya thanks Rajeswari, Chidvilas and Suhas, and Sunitha thanks Ashwyn.

Sathya Prakash Elavarthi
Sunitha Chitrapu

1
UNDERSTANDING MEDIA PRODUCTS, FIRMS AND MARKETS

Firms are central to understanding markets. Understanding how firms come into existence, the choices they have and the strategies they adopt are important to understanding how industry structures evolve over a period of time. However, one cannot understand the structure of the industry by studying an individual firm alone. Examining the conditions at the collective or industry level reveals certain aspects that cannot be understood by studying individual firms. Additionally, understanding of the nature of media products will also throw light on the existence and behaviour of media firms and industries. This chapter uses a multi-pronged approach to examine the nature of media products and firms to gain an in-depth understanding of media industries and media markets.

Understanding the nature of media products

In the economic sense, a "product" is something that is made available to the consumer through a transaction to satisfy a want or a need. In that broad sense, a newspaper, a radio or television broadcast, a film, a book, a music file or a video game are all examples of media products. Media products have some commonalities and differences with other products in the market. The commonality is that it is a product that is bought and sold like others at a given market price. This quality of media products facilitates the study of media economics, as a sub-discipline of microeconomics. The differences of media products with others are many and have been elaborated by many media economists (Picard, Doyle, Albarran et al.) over the years. These differences are based both on the nature of the media product and the way it is perceived by socio-economic actors in the market. It is the study of these differences and their impacts on producers, consumers, media markets, societies and governments that constitute the study of media economics and management. Some of the important ways of

DOI: 10.4324/9781003199212-1

understanding media products and the resulting economic implications are discussed in this chapter.

Public goods

In economics, a public good is defined as one that is non-excludable and non-rivalrous. The nature of a public good is such that no individual can be excluded from its use, and use by one individual does not reduce its availability to others, e.g. national security. In comparison, a private good is rivalrous, in the sense that if one individual consumes it, its value is destroyed for others. Some economists consider media goods as public goods (Wildman, Davies, Picard, Doyle et al.). In such a scenario, should media goods be produced and provided for by the state in the same way it provides for national security and law and order? Media goods are also expected to embody values of free speech and plurality of opinions, and this cannot be ensured by a single producer. In reality, most of the media firms are privately owned, and they exclude non-payers. For a non-excludable and non-rivalrous good such as terrestrial radio or terrestrial broadcasting, the costs of keeping the non-payers from enjoying the good or service is prohibitive. The public good characteristics of media products have implications for financing media operations.

Economics is based on the premise of scarcity. Media economists argue that media output defies the very premise of scarcity. Media inputs suffer different levels of scarcity till the first copy is produced. Once the media product is produced, it does not suffer from scarcity because it is non-rivalrous, i.e., no matter how much a film, song or news story is consumed, it does not get used up completely (Doyle 2002, 10). So, the conventional concept of scarcity does not apply as it would to other private goods, whose value gets diminished on usage. Since consumption by one consumer does not deplete the availability of the product for consumption by others, not making it available to others is considered as welfare loss. For-profit private organisations do not have the incentive to produce public goods because of the free-rider problem. A free-rider problem occurs when consumers enjoy a good or service and do not pay for them, resulting in under-provisioning of resources for production of those goods and services. To circumvent this problem, the creation of public goods like street lighting, law and order and national monuments is often funded by the governments. Broadcast media technologies were non-excludable in their early years, and given their positive externalities, governments considered them as public goods and funded them. In the United States, where ideological opposition to government funding was prevalent, early radio and television broadcasts were funded by advertisers. Over the years, new technologies such as encryption have made exclusion of broadcast products possible. When exclusion is possible, private organisations will try to serve as many fee-paying consumers as possible. Private investments in broadcast technologies increased with the arrival of technologies that increased the degree of excludability and legal provisions such as copyright protection.

Some economists argue that the idea of public goods has to be further refined to make distinctions between pure public goods and marketable public goods. Pure public goods are non-rivalrous and non-excludable, but marketable public goods are non-rival but excludable (Adams and McCormick 1993, 110). They suggest that in the case of marketable public goods, the free-rider problem can be overcome by the new technologies that enable excludability. For media products, rivalness is an intrinsic characteristic, while excludability is external to it. Media content may be non-rival, but the medium by which it is distributed may be a rival good (Gaustad 2010, 250). A newspaper article may be non-rivalrous as it can be shared endlessly, but a printed copy of a newspaper is rivalrous. As the possibilities of building exclusion to greater degrees increase, it becomes difficult to define media goods as public goods in the conventional sense.

Dual product markets

Media products are considered as vehicles for transmission not only for their inherent ideas and experiences, but also for promoting other products by the advertising industry. This instrumental function of media products has significant implications for their packaging and pricing. This also splits the media product market into two interdependent segments: in one segment, media producers produce media goods to get the attention of the audience, and in the second, they trade it as currency with the advertisers. Robert Picard calls the result of this split nature of media products as dual product markets. In economic terms, this makes media products unusual. Media firms create one product but participate in two separate goods and service markets (Picard 1989, 17). This formulation, which had a significant impact on understanding of media markets for quite some time, suggests that media products such as newspapers or TV shows are produced for participation in a content market first and later for participation in the advertising market, with the performance in the first market affecting the performance in the second.

In the content market, media products (newspapers, magazines, books, music or television shows) compete for the attention of the audience. A part of the cost is recovered from the content market in the form of subscription revenues. In the advertising market, media firms compete using the different quantities and qualities of audience attention they have acquired in the content market. (Audience markets will be discussed in detail in Chapter 3.) This market provides media firms with advertising revenues. Media products can choose to operate in both. Sometimes they might participate only in the audience markets in the initial phases of their lifecycle and enter the advertising market in the later stages of their lifecycle. For instance, films are made for audience markets as they face the box office first, and eventually they are broadcast on free-to-air television channels, thereby participating in advertising markets as well. Of course, even at an early stage, films get revenues from theatre advertising and in-film placements, making them participants in advertising markets. While all media products can participate in dual product markets in principle, some may not participate in both for their own strategic reasons. Media firms that focus only on content creation get value for their products by selling them to various packaging firms.

Intangible goods

Media products differ from others in their form and delivery mechanism. All media products involve exchanges of information, ideas and experiences. For instance, a newspaper may give information, opinion or analysis, and a film might provide a certain experience. The primary value of media products is in the ideas and experiences that they provide, which are intangible. This intangible nature of media products is emphasised as an important quality by many media economists. It is argued that this intangible nature provides media products with benefits of scale and scope (Doyle 2002, 13). Economies of scale can be defined as cost advantages that arise with the increased output of a product. As greater quantities of a good are produced, the fixed cost is spread across them, reducing the per unit cost. Economies of scale are present across a range of manufacturing industries involved in assembly line production. In media, scale economies are said to be present in higher propensity due to the intangible nature of the product. Media products are said to enjoy falling marginal costs as the volume of output consumed expands. This happens because the cost of producing an extra unit of a media product is negligible when compared with its first copy cost. For instance, the first copy cost of a film will be very high as it involves costs of casting, production and marketing, but the cost of producing an extra copy falls as thousands of copies are made for theatrical distribution. It has to be noted that scale economies in media products are determined by massive consumption, not by massive production (Arrese 2006, 192). The marginal costs in other media sub-sectors, including publishing, broadcasting and digital media products, are also low, offering them opportunities to reap economies of scale. Apart from economies of scale, media products are also said to enjoy economies of scope. It can be defined as sharing inputs across a range of products to achieve cost efficiencies. When economies of scope are present, it makes sense for a firm to diversify its product range to benefit from lowering of costs by sharing inputs. Media firms can re-combine their inputs and specialist ingredients in many ways, resulting in multi-product production. For instance, Bloomberg specialises in producing financial information, data and analyses. It uses the same information to produce a range of media products across radio, TV, web portals and mobile apps. If all these products are to be produced by different firms, their collective cost will be much higher than the total cost to the combined firm, in this case Bloomberg.

However, economies of scale and scope are not unlimited; at a certain stage, diseconomies do arise. To continue with the example of film, initially the marginal cost of producing an extra unit will fall as the output expands. But, after a certain stage, the marginal costs will equal average costs and producing extra units beyond this point will lead to diseconomies of scale. In theory, recombining ingredients of media products and sharing resources in production seems possible and would lead to economies of scope. In practice, when a diversified firm attempts to integrate operations of its newspaper and TV broadcast simultaneously, it is not easy and involves the costs of coordinating these functions. This will lead to diseconomies of scope after a certain stage. More about economies of scale, scope and diseconomies is discussed in Chapters 2 and 6.

The intangible nature of media products also results in some negative consequences. It is very difficult to forecast demand and make pricing decisions for intangible goods. The peculiarities that intangible goods embody render scores of traditional assessment mechanisms for transactions and pricing inadequate (Arrese 2006, 192). Since media products are intangible, the monetisation process is built around delivery mechanisms, which make media products tangible; in other words, intangible goods need to be embedded in tangible forms to make it available for exclusive consumption. Of late, digital media has resolved this problem to a certain extent but has also increased the problem of piracy.

Bundled goods

The practice of offering several products together as a package for a single price is called bundling. Bundling is accepted as a rational strategy in product markets that enjoy economies of scale and scope and in markets that suffer from high consumer acquisition costs. Since media products are intangible, and since they can be packaged in various combinations, it has become a convention for media companies to offer their products in bundles. And since seeking out listeners, viewers and readers for single products is a risky and expensive business proposition, media companies adopt bundling. A newspaper publisher or a broadcaster packages various components on a daily basis for their readers and viewers. Films, popular music and video games are initially released as single products, but as they mature, they are bundled to realise their residuary value.

The idea of value for a single media product gets extremely complicated in a bundled environment. For instance, a newspaper is a bundle of news, opinions, editorials, cartoons, columns, etc. The market price is for the bundle as a whole and not for the components. The advertising insertions can be based on both the bundle as a whole or on a subset of the bundle. Generally, the individual items in the bundle seem to be less significant in the overall valuation of the media product, but the cost involved in making each of these single items is clear and significant. Some of these individual items are produced by the newspaper firm, while some are procured from others (syndication, freelancing, expert opinions, etc.). A media packaging firm will have definite bundling costs that are not charged directly to the consumer alone, but absorbed by the advertisers as well. These complicated cost and price arrangements have consequences for the performance and profitability of firms in media markets.

The advent of digital information goods with very low marginal costs can make bundling hundreds or even thousands of unrelated goods a profitable strategy (Bakos and Brynjolfsson 1999, 1.614). According to Bakos and Brynjolfsson (1999), consumer's valuation for a collection of goods typically has a probability distribution with a lower price variance per good compared to the valuations for the individual goods. Pricing the bundle optimally is a challenge, and it depends on the size of the bundle, nature and marginal costs of its components and the value perception among consumers. A multiproduct aggregator may achieve higher profits and greater efficiency through bundling strategy than by selling them individually. Bundling seems to confer size-based advantages that are different from scale, scope and network effects. Some of these aspects about bundling will be discussed in Chapter 8 on digital media.

Uncertain markets

Demand uncertainty is endemic to media markets. No media product is similar to the earlier one, and this makes the consumer response difficult to predict. A film by the same creative team might not generate financial returns like their earlier film. Production of media products is not based on demand forecast, as in the steel or cement industries. Uncertainty in demand affects firms as they cannot decide how much to produce and at what price. When price, quantity to be produced and the revenues that can be realised cannot be estimated, resource allocation processes of firms and the industry are affected. Media firms are forced to work in such uncertain demand conditions. To overcome this problem, they use various strategies such as promotion and marketing, the star system and attempts towards control of distribution channels.

Theoretically, in free market economies, most decisions concerning resource allocation are made through the price discovery mechanism enabled by the forces of demand and supply. Price discovery happens in the marketplace through the interaction between buyers and sellers. According to Doyle, the relationship between the price and resource allocation in the media is somewhat unusual (2002, 11). Many media products and services do not involve direct payment from the audience/viewer. Many media products are subsidised by advertisers. For example, a newspaper is partly subsidised by advertisers, and some television programmes are completely subsidised by advertisers. So, the price of a media product for the consumer will not fully reflect the cost of producing it. When price does not act as a direct link between producers and consumers, it affects resource allocation and funding mechanisms in the industry.

Understanding market structures in media industry

Media firms and media industries

In classical economic theory, production is defined as conversion of land, labour and capital into goods and services. Firms are defined as establishments where production is carried out. Industries are defined as a grouping of many firms producing a commodity for the same market.

Features of products or services, the process of production and the substitutability of products or services from the viewpoint of consumers are used as prime criteria for grouping firms into an industry. In this case, a media firm can be defined as one that is involved in one or all stages of the media value chain—production, packaging and distribution of media content. This definition is broad enough to ignore minor variations among media firms, but it is narrow enough to exclude fundamental variations that distinguish it from other industries. These firms can be further divided into sub-segments for easier understanding and analysis. So, rather than thinking of a single media industry, we can think of a number of media industries that include publishing, film production, television broadcasting, radio broadcasting and digital media industries. Even though emerging technologies of convergence are blurring clear market boundaries, these markets continue to exist. Media firms can be further classified on the basis of the form they take; for instance, in the case of publishing, they can be classified as book publishers, newspaper publishers and magazine publishers. In the case of television broadcasting, they can be classified as general entertainment channels (GECs) and niche channels for sports, music, movies, adventure, spirituality and so on. Language and region are also some of the variables by which media industries can be segmented. Each of these ways of segmenting industries will help in analysing demand, competition and performance at various levels and stages in these industries.

Market structures in media

Market structure is a theoretical construct used to explain the overarching economic framework in which firms operate. Substitutability of the products, competition among sellers and entry and exit barriers in a given market are the important determinants that differentiate one market structure from another.

Neoclassical market models have been the dominant criteria for explaining market structures in the last century. Even though some competing heterodox models exist, they have not displaced the neoclassical way of understanding markets. Neoclassical economics is based on the premise of the existence of rational actors, information equity, rational allocation and utility maximisation.

In this model, all the actors involved are rational actors—be it individual consumers or firms. The individual consumer is interested in maximising her utility from consuming a particular good, while the firm is interested in maximising its profits. Utility increases till a point of inflection at which diminishing marginal utility or diminishing marginal productivity will start. The model assumes that all actors are optimally informed and act rationally to the extent that resource allocation at the market level adjusts itself to the changes in demand and supply.

Based on this framework, neoclassical economics classifies market structures into: (1) Perfect Competition, (2) Monopoly, (3) Oligopoly and (4) Monopolistic Competition. We examine each of these models next.

1   *Perfect Competition*: The construct of perfect competition is at the heart of neoclassical market models. Perfect competition is modelled as an ideal

market structure, and the rest of the models are explained on the basis of deviations from this structure. In a perfectly competitive market, there are many firms producing homogenous and perfectly substitutable products. No firm has control over the market, and this is reflected in every firm being a price taker, i.e., it has to accept the price at which market transactions can take place and is unable to set a price, because buyers have plenty of alternative sellers to choose from. If the firm chooses to offer a lower price, then other sellers are able to offer the same. All the consumers are optimally informed and there are no information asymmetries. This market structure does not have entry and exit barriers. Changes in demand or supply are taken care of by the free entry and exit of firms. Given these conditions, the market price is determined by uncoordinated actions of independent agents, i.e., buyers and sellers. This model cannot be tested empirically because such market conditions do not exist; however, this model is regarded as an ideal, so that policy makers can make policies to nudge inefficient market structures closer to this ideal.

2 *Monopoly*: The theoretical model of monopoly is conceived as the opposite of perfect competition. This market structure has a single seller, there are no close substitutes for the product and market structure imposes high barriers of entry. Since the firm's output equals market output, the firm involved will be a price maker, i.e., the firm is able to set the price of its choice since buyers do not have any other options.

Monopoly situations in media arise due to factors such as technology, or government policy or business practices. For instance, the IMAX Corporation controls film production and distribution in this large screen format through its proprietary technology. The Government of India did not allow private players in the broadcasting sector, making television and radio broadcasting government monopolies for decades. If a broadcaster wins the bid for telecast rights of the cricket World Cup, they have the monopoly over broadcasting that event. There could be many other examples such as the lone film theatre in a small town or a lone cable distributor in a geographical area.

3 *Monopolistic Competition*: This market structure is characterised with many firms producing differentiated products, but products that are not perfect substitutes. In this market a consumer will not find a perfect substitute in case of increase in price. However, if the price rise is too steep, she can move to a not-so-perfect substitute. Firms behave like monopolies in the short run, but in long run, other firms will bridge the product differentiation and reduce the market power of a firm, i.e., its ability to set the price. Entry into this market is not very difficult. Each firm has some leeway in pricing its product but will have to be conscious of the substitutability of other firm's products in the market in case of dramatic price changes.

For instance, the mobile TV distribution market, can be considered as a monopolistic market. All the players in the market offer a bundle of channels centred on their own app. Hotstar, Ditto TV, Tata Sky Mobile, SonyLIV, YuppTV and Airtel Pocket TV are some of the leading TV content distributors on mobile platform in India. Each of them has a slightly differentiated mix of content on offer at different prices. Some have sports as the key differentiator, while others have soaps or films. If one player gains viewership share by distributing a certain kind of content, others will try to bridge this gap by acquiring similar content.

4   *Oligopoly*: In this market structure, there are a few sellers with either homogenous or differentiated products. The behaviour of firms in oligopoly depends on the number of sellers and the substitutability of products. Depending on how few the sellers are, the price competition can be moderate to that of high intensity. Entry barriers can range from difficult to very difficult depending on the seller concentration. Oligopolistic markets are known for raising artificial barriers to entry for protecting their market power in the long run. Sometimes, oligopolistic firms also collude, forming cartels for windfall profits and for restricting entry of new firms.

   Many media firms operate in an oligopolistic market structure. If we take the national English-language newspaper market in India, the important players are *The Times of India*, *Hindustan Times*, *The Hindu*, *The Telegraph*, *Deccan Chronicle*, and the *Tribune*. Even the Hindi General Entertainment Channel (GEC) segment can be considered as an oligopoly market. Even though there are around 20 Hindi GECs, only 6 have significant market share. Between them Star Utsav, Star Plus, Zee Anmol, Sony Pal, Sony SAB and Dangal figure as the top 6 among the top 10 channels, in the channel rankings given by Broadcast Audience Research Council of India (BARC), making them oligopolies (based on BARC weekly data, Week 39).

Beyond neoclassical models

The basic premises of neoclassical economics—i.e., rational actors, information equity, rational allocation and maximising utility—have been contested by many economists. To overcome the limitations of neoclassical premises, economists have attempted new ways of understanding markets in general and media markets in particular. In a media market with information asymmetries, the theoretical possibility of a rational actor is difficult to fulfil. Television viewers do not objectively go about maximising their subjective utility. In fact, it is not possible to understand the consequences of watching different programmes with certainty for any viewer. A viewer can only have a certain set of expectations based on previous experiences.

   Heterodox approaches such as behavioural economics, transaction cost economics, information economics and evolutionary economics are being increasingly used to explain and understand media markets given the limitations of neoclassical approaches.

Market structure and firm behaviour—*theoretical models and their limitations*

Many models have been proposed to explain the relationship between the market structure and its impact on the behaviour of firms in an industry.

SCP and RBV models

Edward Mason in the 1930s proposed the Structure–Conduct–Performance Model (SCP). Improvements were later made by his student Joseph Bain in the 1950s. The model, based on industrial organisation (IO) concepts, proposes that market structures within which media firms operate affect how individual media firms organise their resources and conduct their business affairs in the industry. Market structures also affect the choices consumers can make and the strategies that competitors will adopt. This is a short-term proposition as the market structures themselves are bound to change in the medium and long terms. The SCP framework suggests a linear relationship between the structure of the industry and its impact on the conduct of a firm operating within this structure and their performance.

For instance, if a media firm is operating in a perfectly competitive market structure, then it will produce undifferentiated goods, it will be a price taker and it will neither face nor worry about raising barriers to entry. Since hardly any media firm operates in a perfectly competitive market, it is difficult to demonstrate the SCP framework in this market condition. Media sub-sectors like niche television broadcasters and niche magazines come close to the monopolistic competition model, i.e., they produce differentiated goods, price their goods aware of possible substitutability and constantly reorient product and pricing policies to avoid new entrants eating into their market share.

Economists agree that most media markets fall close to oligopolistic structures. General entertainment channels across language markets, national and regional mainstream newspapers, general-interest national magazines, FM stations in urban markets, and English-language newspapers are examples of oligopoly market structures in India. Given this market structure, a firm operating in these markets will compete fiercely on both product and pricing fronts, raise barriers and collaborate or collude if necessary, to avoid competition. Since the content is not highly differentiated, firms in oligopoly markets tend to position and market themselves aggressively.

Since the SCP framework is built on industrial economics and industrial organisation concepts, it suffers from the deficiencies associated with them. Some economists argue that structure of the market cannot completely explain the behaviour of firms. In fact, the behaviour of certain firms can sometimes alter the existing market structure. Media economists have come to agree that structure is not as static and unidirectional as suggested by SCP framework (Wirth and Bloch 1995, 24).

While the SCP approach emphasises on exogenous factors, the resources-based view (RBV) approach emphasises on the internal resources of a firm and its ability to harness them. The RBV approach builds on the assumption that each firm is a collection of unique resources that enable it to conceive and implement strategies. In this approach, firms discover assets and skills that are unique to their organisation and use it to build competitive advantage in the market. According to RBV, four specific attributes—value, rareness, non-substitutability and inimitability—must work in tandem to increase performance (Chan-Olmsted 2006, 164). The resource might have value, rareness and non-substitutability, but inimitability has to be ensured by building some barrier for enjoying sustained competitive advantage.

Apart from the two dominant approaches of SCP and RBV, other approaches, such as ecological niche theory and game theory, are used to explain the strategic behaviour of firms in the media industry.

Ownership patterns and firm behaviour—alternative models

Neoclassical economics assumes that every decision taken by firms is to maximise profits, especially in relation to its costs. This is a simplified and caricatured explanation of a firm's behaviour. When a firm starts operating in an industry or market, it faces too many complexities for it to adopt the singular goal of profit maximisation. The legal, moral, cultural and social spheres, in which media firms operate, make them work towards objectives which may not always result in monetary profits. Many modern-day firms have realised that the profit maximisation model works only in the short run and have replaced it with a variety of strategies for long-term benefits. These include the sales maximisation model for firms aimed at increasing sales or market share, growth maximisation models aimed at expansion of operations and acquisition of assets, the present value model aimed at maximising the owner's wealth, the managerial utility model which suggests that the ownership and management dichotomy in modern-day corporations results in managers sometimes pursuing strategies which are not necessarily intended to increase profits for the owners. All these models suggest that at some level profit is the main goal, be it sales maximisation, growth maximisation or present value maximisation. Only the managerial utility model suggests the possibility of the manager—an agent making self-serving moves that can affect the owner or investors. But modern corporations work with the help of experts and on the principle of delegation, which makes the agent a necessity, and this delegation is done with the intention of expanding operations and profits. So, most of these models suggest that a firm's behaviour is to work towards the goal of profit using different paths.

There are many exceptions to this in the case of media industries. In the case of not-for-profit firms, whose stated goals are other than profit, the firm's behaviour might be driven by other objectives. Media firms may have alternative goals like philanthropy and the pursuit of public or political influence (Doyle 2002, 5). For instance, public broadcasters provide content generated according to their own guidelines and not according to market demand. Another exception is religious and evangelical broadcasting. Religious and evangelical channels like Astha, Sanskar, Miraclenet and Peace TV are funded through donations and grants, and revenue generation is not a primary goal. Similarly, the proliferation of television news channels, despite the shrinking advertising pie, fragmentation of audiences and low take-off in subscription revenues, cannot be explained by the profit maximisation goal. It can be argued that investments in news channels are made with an eye on political influence despite their inability to realise financial returns.

Factors affecting market structures in media industries

This section will discuss the factors that determine market structures. In the case of media firms and industries, technology and public policy have been two major determinants of market structures. Whenever a new technology enters the market, or whenever a major policy decision is taken, market structures change. These changes sometimes result in consolidation of market power, and they sometimes enable more democratic market structures.

Policy barriers in media have been fading away in the last three decades due to liberalisation, privatisation and globalisation. While we still have certain restrictions on the ownership of news media, the rest of the media industry segments have been opened to global investment and competition. Technological innovations over a period of time have been reducing entry barriers in some areas. For instance, desktop publishing has reduced initial production costs in publishing and enabled many players to enter this industry.

Technological changes have affected the economics of television. Two important technological changes affecting television content distribution have taken place in the last few decades: (1) digital compression techniques, and (2) proliferation of distribution platforms. These developments have reduced traditional entry barriers of access to spectrum and high input costs. The expansion in the delivery methods has meant a shifting of focus from the means of distribution to content creation. In a multi-channel environment, the success of a broadcaster depends mostly on attractive programming. The value of content and content producers has risen significantly. The second important technological development in television broadcasting is encryption and decoding which allows addressability, i.e., the presence of the set top box in the consumer's home allows the cable or satellite distributor to control access to content. These technologies enable direct payment from the consumers.

With the arrival of digital media technologies, the way content is distributed and consumed is changing across a range of media sub-sectors. The value chains of publishing, music and video sectors have gone through a sea change after the arrival of distribution technologies online and in mobile platforms.

Lifecycle of media industries—*sunrise industries, mature industries, declining industries*

The idea of lifecycle for industries is based on the evolutionary philosophy that industries also have a lifecycle of birth and death. Industries that are at the beginning stage of the lifecycle are labelled as sunrise industries, as the market sees a lot of future potential in them. The ones at their peak performance stage are labelled as mature industries, and industries at the end of their lifecycle with diminishing future potential are labelled as declining industries. The concept of industry lifecycle comes from organisational ecology (OE) studies. Organisational ecology is interested in studying the conditions under which organisations emerge, grow and die.

Industries in their emergent phase and growth phase can be considered sunrise industries. They are characterised by innovation and large entry of firms since barriers to entry are limited. Despite the existence of competition, most of them will have good sales and profits. This phase cannot continue for long as the industry soon surpasses the carrying capacity and some of the firms in the industry try to dominate the market through standardisation and scaling up. This process leads to consolidation or a shakeout in the industry. After one shakeout or a series of shakeouts, the industry enters the mature phase. Mature industries are characterised by limited but tough competition. As innovations reduce due to standardisation, most of the competition will be around price, quality, and product differentiation. Many small firms will exit the market at this stage as they fail to compete with the big players. In the long run, shift in consumer demand due to changing tastes and product substitution due to technological advancements reduce demand for firms in the mature industries. Slowly, the industry growth rate slows down, and the industry enters into a declining phase. Declining industries are characterised by almost no entry of new firms, low investments and low profitability. A firm entering the industry would have to do lifecycle planning. Knowing the position of an industry in the industry lifecycle helps to understand the dynamics of market structure and the entry, exit and survival patterns of firms (Kranenburg and Hogenbirk 2006, 326)

In the global media context, digital media industries can be regarded as sunrise industries. Companies like Google and Facebook can be considered as sunrise companies. Television broadcasting can be considered as an example of a mature sub-segment in the media industry, while book publishing and newspaper publishing in the western markets can be regarded as a declining industry. Declining does not mean a complete end or cessation. Sometimes declining industries are revived by new technologies in a new form. From the Guttenberg Bible in the 1450s, book publishing has survived for more than 500 years. Even though hard copy publishing is on the decline, new technologies like audio books and e-books are reviving publishing in newer ways. Even record companies, who faced decline in physical form, have reinvented themselves with online music retailing and subscription streaming. Although not a part of the modern media industry, circus companies and theatre companies are clear examples of declining or dying industries, as both changing tastes and technological substitution has affected them.

Industry lifecycles can be at different stages for different markets and geographies in the same industry. For instance, newspaper publishing is a mature industry in India with peak performance, while it is a declining industry in Europe and North America. Some language publishing markets in the Indian context are still in a growth stage, as new firms are entering the sector.

Firms in declining industries use different strategies to survive and to profitably exit from the industry. No new firms want to enter the declining industry, while the existing firms may want to exit the industry. If the assets of the firm in a declining industry cannot be redeployed for other purposes, they are regarded as sunk costs.

This chapter has provided a varied approach to understanding the nature of media products and the resulting implications for understanding media markets. It has further examined the firm's behaviour based on its internal resources and in response to its external environment using IO and OE approaches. The next chapter will build on this by providing conceptual understanding of revenues, costs, demand, output and pricing in media industries.

References

Adams, R. D., and McCormick, K. (1993). The traditional distinction between public and private goods needs to be expanded, not abandoned. *Journal of Theoretical Politics*, 5(1), 109–116.

Arrese, A. (2006). Issues in media product management. In A. B. Albarran, S. M. Chan-Olmsted, and M. O. Wirth (Eds.), *Handbook of Media Management and Economics*. New York: Routledge.

Bakos, Y., and Brynjolfsson, E. (1999). Bundling information goods: Pricing, profits and efficiency. *Management Science*, 45(12), 1.613–1.630.

BARC weekly data, week 39. Retrieved November 27, 2020, from www.barcindia.co.in/data-insights

Chan-Olmsted, S. M. (2006). Issues in strategic management. In A. B. Albarran, S. M. Chan-Olmsted, and M. O. Wirth (Eds.), *Handbook of Media Management and Economics*. Routledge: New York.

Doyle, G. (2002). *Understanding Media Economics*. London: Sage Publications.

Gaustad, T. (2010). The problem of excludability for media and entertainment products in new electronic market channels. *Electronic Markets*, 12(4), 248–251.

Kranenburg, H. V., and Hogenbirk, A. (2006). Issues in market structure. In A. B. Albarran, S. M. Chan-Olmsted, and M. O. Wirth (Eds.), *Handbook of Media Management and Economics*. New York: Routledge.

Wirth, M. O., and Bloch, H. (1995). Industrial organization theory and media industry analysis. *Journal of Media Economics*, 8(2), 15–26.

2

MEDIA FIRMS

Revenues, costs, demand, supply and pricing

Demand, supply, revenues, costs and prices are interconnected economic aspects. When it comes to media products, there are many product-specific, structural and environmental factors that influence each of these interconnected aspects individually and as a whole. By examining revenues, costs, demand, supply and prices in the specific context of media markets, this chapter attempts to understand the special circumstances in which media products are produced, priced and supplied.

Revenue streams in media industries

Analysing the revenues of a firm or an industry is a way to understand that sector. New firms planning to enter an industry will use reports by market research firms or do their own homework to assess the revenue potential of the markets they wish to enter. It is important not only for the new firms to identify viable and sustainable revenue streams, but also for investors and creditors to assess the rate of return and associated risks for deciding on the investment.

The dual-product nature of the media product means it has two primary sets of revenues. The first set comes directly from consumer markets, i.e., through subscriptions, and the second set from advertising markets. However, there are firms which are completely dependent on only one source. For instance, book publishers depend completely on the cover price, while free newspapers depend completely on advertising. Many media firms try to get their revenues from both sources. Firms operating in the newspaper and broadcast markets get their revenues from both subscription and advertising. The ratio of advertising to subscription revenues differs by media segment and media product. In 2019, the television broadcasting segment made INR 714 billion in total revenues, of which subscription revenues were INR 463 billion (65%) and advertising

DOI: 10.4324/9781003199212-2

revenues were 251 billion (35%) (KPMG 2019, 56). Within television broadcasting, the advertising share of total revenues is high for news broadcasters, as they are free to air. In 2019, the print sector, including newspapers and magazines made INR 333 billion in total revenues, of which advertising revenues were INR 221 billion (66%) and circulation revenues were INR 112 billion (34%) (KPMG 2019, 68). The sources of revenue have implications for the nature of the media product, competition and the structure of the market. Firms operating in media markets which are primarily driven by advertising revenues tend to move towards oligopoly. These markets with varying degrees of concentration also pose challenges to regulators in terms of consumer welfare and diversity of content (Doyle 2002, 74). The subscription system yields the results that reflect the cost of scarce resources in alternative uses, and therefore tends to solve the problem of efficiency in resource allocation (Minasian 1964, 76). However, demand forecasting and the costs of acquiring and managing subscriptions will be high, and non-paying and low-paying consumers might be excluded, leading to welfare loss.

Revenues also differ according to the nature of the product. Revenue sources for products like films with longer product lifecycles are different from those of daily newspapers and broadcast news which have very short product lifecycles. Even though most of the revenues for films are generated in the first few weeks of box office release, a variety of windows ranging from overseas box office, pay-per-view, home video, subscription-based broadcast, free-to-air broadcast, SVOD and merchandising ensure a flow of revenues for months and in some cases years for successful films. Revenues for newspapers and news broadcasters are based as much on the format and ratings as they are on the content, which is highly variable and has a short shelf life.

Media firms can increase their revenues in many ways. For instance, they can increase their subscription prices to increase their revenues; however, this move could affect their price competitiveness in an already competitive environment. Media firms can also differentiate their content to increase revenues from consumers. This strategy will be constrained if competitors offer close substitutes (Kind et al. 2009, 1112). Media firms with exclusive rights over content such as sports can make significant revenues from consumers as they are not substitutable. Other options include increases in their advertising prices or advertising inventories. Increases in advertising prices affect price competitiveness in advertising markets, while raising advertising inventory results in dilution of the media vehicle. When the number of advertisements is high in a media product, especially in television and cable industries, it affects the consumer experience. It will also affect the return on investment by the viewers. A newspaper has to be conscious of the news–to–advertising space ratio. A TV broadcaster can have only a fixed amount of commercial minutes within each hour of programming; beyond this a media firm cannot increase the quantity as it will dilute the value both to the consumers and advertisers. Given the inter-connectedness of content and advertising markets, closer substitutability between media products makes advertising revenue relatively more important, whereas a large number of media products increase the relative importance of direct payments from the audience (Kind et al. 2009, 1123).

New technologies or policies that disrupt existing value chains give rise to greater uncertainty in revenues. Performance in these periods of uncertainty or transition holds the key to the success of a firm in the long run. Currently, as new media sectors are making advances, legacy media businesses are responding to the challenges of shrinking market shares and revenues. As media usage patterns change, advertisers follow them, disrupting the existing arrangements of value generation. New distribution technologies have made media goods excludable, bringing in the possibility of pay revenues. For instance, addressable set top boxes and satellite dishes allow pay-per-view channels that allow broadcasters new sources of revenues directly from consumers compared to earlier means of free-to-air broadcasting. But the cost of adapting these new technologies affects the firm's balance sheet in the short run. Table 2.1 outlines traditonal and new revenue sources of some existing media products.

Cost structures in the media industries

After assessing potential revenues, a media firm has to assess the costs involved for optimal allocation of resources. In economic theory, costs are classified in many different ways. One of the important ways of classifying a firm's costs is based on the length of time in which they occur, as short-run and long-run costs. In the long run, all costs are considered to be variable. Firms are always considered to function in the short run, where some input costs are fixed and some input costs are variable. In the short run, fixed costs are those overheads that have to be incurred irrespective of the level of output. Variable costs increase or decrease with the level of output. Marginal cost is defined as the cost of producing one more unit of the good.

Since some costs are variable in the short run, firms try to figure out the level of output at the most cost-efficient level. Measuring the cost elasticity of output helps in this process. Elasticity of cost measures the percentage of change in total cost due to a percentage of change in output.

$$\text{Elasticity of Cost} = \frac{\text{Percentage of Change in Total Cost}}{\text{Percentage of change in Output}}$$

When cost elasticity equals 1, it is considered to be the most cost-efficient level of output. If there is no significant change in cost due to change in output, then it is considered to be cost inelastic. If changes in cost lead to changes in output, then it is considered to be cost elastic. Cost elasticity is very high for media firms. Since media products are intangible in nature, their initial production costs tend to be very high, while their marginal costs tend to be very low.

TABLE 2.1 Revenue Streams in Media Sub-Sectors

Media Firms	Traditional Revenue Sources	New Revenue Sources
Book Publishing	Printed book sales (bookstore and online), e-book sales, audio book sales	Advertising in e-books, pay-per-use, licencing
Newspaper Publishing	Subscriptions, advertising, events	Micropayments online, digital subscriptions
Magazine Publishing	Subscriptions, advertising, events	Digital subscriptions
TV Content Producers	Commissioned sales, Syndication, Home Video	TVOD*, SVOD*, Advertising share of streaming with online aggregators
TV Broadcasters	Advertising, Subscriptions	VoD, Digital Subscriptions, Advertising share of streaming with online aggregators
TV Distribution	Subscription Fees, Advertising, Carriage fees	Digital Subscriptions
Radio Broadcasters	Advertising	Digital subscriptions
Films	Box office, broadcast rights, audio rights, home video	TVOD, SVOD
Gaming	Console sales, game sales, royalties, rentals	Online advertising, Freemium, Advergaming, microtransactions, games with lock-in features

Source: Authors

*TVOD—Transaction Video on Demand
*SVOD—Subscription Video on Demand

As their output increases, their total costs come down significantly, providing increasing returns to scale and scope.

Economies of scale in the media industry

As discussed in Chapter 1, economies of scale are defined as cost advantages related to increased scale of operations. When the cost of providing an extra unit of a good falls as the scale of output expands, economies of scale are said to be present. For instance, in the automobile industry, as more units of cars are sold, the average cost of production comes down. In most sub-sectors of the media industry, marginal costs tend to be very low. As more viewers tune in to a broadcaster or as more readers purchase a copy of the newspaper, or as more people access a website, the average cost goes down. This results in lower costs and higher profits for these firms. When economies of scale are present in an industry, bigger firms will have lesser average costs than the smaller ones. This benefit incentivises firms to make efforts to increase their production to obtain the cost benefits associated with scale.

This concept of scale was developed in the context of industrial economics and does pose some problems when applied to media firms. Since scale economies in media products are determined by massive consumption, not by massive production (Arrese 2006, 192), it has to be applied differently in the case of media products. Consumption (audience production) in media products can be verified only in hindsight and not when the output is produced. At best media firms have to estimate the level of consumption required at the most cost-efficient level. For instance, a broadcaster should be able to estimate the level and quality of viewership to measure the cost-efficiency of their programme acquisition.

Economies of scope in the media industry

Economies of scope are also associated with the concept of cost advantages. Unlike economies of scale, in this case cost advantages are achieved by producing two or more products together. The savings of the firm increase as a range of firm's products are produced in increased quantities. Savings are achieved with multi-product production through input sharing among a group of products, and through joint distribution and sale. For instance, when a newspaper house starts a broadcasting venture and a web portal, it can use common editorial inputs across these ventures. It can also save costs by centralising administrative, marketing and sales functions. When economies of scope are present in an industry, the total costs of a multi-product firm will be less than the sum of costs of single-product firms (Doyle 2002, 15). This possibility drives media firms to produce a range of products by diversifying into allied areas.

Diseconomies of scale and scope in the media industry

Economies of scale and scope are not unlimited. At a certain level of output, they hit a plateau, and from there diseconomies of scale and scope kick in. When diseconomies of scale appear, the firm has the option to cut back on production to ensure that cost efficiencies and profitability remain at the optimum level. Diseconomies of scale happen at the product and firm levels, while diseconomies of scope are evident only at the firm level. The point at which diseconomies of scale kick in depend on the marginal costs involved in the media segments. The marginal costs are higher in publishing compared to radio, television broadcasting and web operations. So, diseconomies of scale come in earlier for newspaper, magazine and book publishers, while they come much later for broadcasters and new media firms. Diseconomies of scope happen when there are cost inefficiencies in joint production and distribution of multiple products. When diseconomies of scope appear, the multiproduct firm can either discontinue the products that are contributing to inefficiencies or spin off some of the products into different units to maintain profitability.

There are many instances of diversified media firms shutting operations of some units as they become unviable. For example, The Zee Group closed its Gujarati entertainment and news operations in 2009, citing losses. Similarly, Turner Broadcasting shut down its Hindi GEC, Imagine TV in 2012 due to poor performance.

Baumol's "cost disease" in media industries

The previous sections discussed cost efficiencies related to media products and firms. Some economists point out that there are severe cost inefficiencies as well in media industries, especially due to their rising labour costs. American economist William J. Baumol, in his theory of cost disease, suggests that the creative arts, education and health sectors face increasing real costs of inputs without productivity gains. He terms them as victims of cost disease and suggests the use of public grants and subsidies as a means to overcome this problem. Many media economists have worked on elaborating this proposition in the last few decades and have also worked on gathering empirical evidence. Baumol's proposition is based on the premise that in spite of technological progress, certain types of labour cannot be replaced. The irreplaceable labour in the context of media can be regarded as the creative inputs from talented human resources such as directors, writers, lyricists, singers, actors and so on.

Creative inputs are original ideas, concepts, actions and inductive solutions to ill-defined problems. Creative inputs are provided by creative labour, which is assumed to be irreplaceable by machinery (Preston and Sparviero 2009, 243). Since there is no possibility of productivity gains due to an increase in labour efficiency in creative industries, output can be increased only by increasing labour input. For instance, desktop publishing (DTP) has reduced costs and the drudgery in publishing, but it cannot improve the quality of writing, which is still dependent on the individual or team of writers. When we are discussing productivity in the content stage, quality is a more important parameter than quantity. The cost of creative inputs as a proportion of total costs will keep increasing because creative inputs cannot be standardised to provide benefits of scale.

The cost disease applies only to the content creation aspect of creative industries and not to the distribution phase, where innovative technologies have progressively increased productivity gains. The lack of productivity gains in the content phase is more than compensated for by the productivity gains in the distribution and exhibition stages. So, the churn will be very high for media firms, especially to those firms that operate only in content markets. In this context, the term "churn" refers to the number of new firms that are created and the number of firms that are closed down in the content markets. They can survive better by following a portfolio approach at the production stage and by diversifying into the packaging and distribution stages to get scale benefits. The portfolio approach is followed by successful film production companies in Hollywood, while bouquetisation is followed by television broadcasters in India. Bouquetisation refers to the practice of owning a range of channels that cater to different age groups and taste groups. Successful content enjoys scale benefits at the distribution stage, while unsuccessful content would suffer losses in all stages. Given the uncertainty, the other model figured out by media production firms is to control the delivery phase and force feed their own content into the system, as is done by some large, vertically integrated media companies. This is not considered to be a fair business practice and might attract the attention of competition commissions. For instance, Hollywood majors are vertically integrated and hence enjoy assured distribution, unlike independents. Even in the Indian context, some Bollywood majors, big players in the Tamil and Telugu film industries, are accused of controlling the distribution phase to ensure their profitability.

Clustering in media industries and cost efficiencies

Clusters are geographic concentrations of interconnected firms which compete, cooperate and innovate. Even though clustering is an important feature of many other industries, it is a defining feature of media industries. Globally, media industries are characterised by heavy geographical concentration. Filmmaking in Hollywood and Mumbai, and publishing in New York, London and Delhi, are all examples of media clusters. These clusters can agglomerate at various levels in different media sub-sectors. There could be global hubs and regional hubs. While Hollywood and Mumbai (Bollywood) are global hubs for film production, Chennai, Hyderabad, Bengaluru, Kochi and Kolkata are regional film production hubs.

Clustering in media helps improve the productivity of individual firms. Media clusters promote and improve production of entertainment and content by connecting producers through private and public partnerships, networks and projects, thus making media production more efficient (Karlsson and Picard 2011, 4). The advantages of co-location are very high for content firms because they work through labour pooling across projects and firms. For an industry that suffers from escalating human resource costs, this seems to be a coping mechanism.

The success of media firms depends on their ability to continuously churn out new products. So it becomes critical for the media firms to actively monitor their competitors and improve their own content. The presence of media firms in a cluster enables them to actively monitor competitors. This stimulates competition, imitation and ultimately innovation. Another major benefit of clusters is the rapid diffusion of new ideas and technologies due to constant and face-to-face interaction between firms. Clusters also attract new talent and entrepreneurs due to the ready availability of infrastructure. Clustering also provides media firms with the advantage of visibility and branding. On the flipside, any negative report on some firms can have an impact on the collective reputation of the cluster.

Clusters will have large integrated firms, small specialist firms, ancillary firms, subcontracting firms, independents and freelancers. They develop a mutually beneficial relationship over a period of time with an intricate web of transactions. Cluster agglomeration can be caused by various factors. Clustering of media industries in Mumbai happened because most of the media businesses were dependent on advertising. These media firms wanted to be present in Mumbai, the financial nerve centre of India, so that executives who take advertising decisions were aware of them. Since the 1990s, Bollywood's sales and exports have been skyrocketing, and the cluster has built widespread synergies with TV, pop music, computer games and advertising (Lorenzen and Mudambi 2010, 7–11). In the animation industry, cluster agglomeration has happened in East Asia, especially in the Philippines due to the availability of cheaper outsourced labour.

Governments all over the world have tried to create clusters around talented human resources, be it through the creation of IT parks, financial districts, education districts or media clusters. Governments provide tax concessions and infrastructure to enable the development of clusters. Governments may have various reasons to encourage clusters, such as job creation, regional development and indigenous content creation. The idea of a Dubai Media City as a Free Economic Zone stems from this form of thinking. When the Dubai Media City was started in 2001, it was planned as an ecosystem where media and allied firms could thrive. By 2001, a plethora of high-profile multinationals and other foreign companies, including Microsoft, Dell, Reuters and the BBC, were locating themselves in the new Dubai Internet City and Dubai Media City (Davidson 2009, 9). Earlier clusters happened due to historical developments, but of late clusters are being developed through government policies to develop certain regions. Besides infrastructure and tax concessions, media firms also need a liberal atmosphere to grow and thrive. In the Middle East region, Dubai is perceived to be reasonably liberal, and that has helped it to emerge as a leader in media services.

One view is that technological convergence reduces the need for agglomeration. Developments in ICTs could reduce the need for face-to-face interactions and therefore the need to co-locate. However, since the content production stage involves irreplaceable labour, media companies could continue to enjoy the cost benefits of co-location.

Determining output of media products—*production function* and *diminishing marginal productivity*

Determining how much to produce is a big challenge in the case of media products. In economic theory, the relationship between inputs and output is defined by the *production function*. Manufacturing firms take into account factor costs and the substitutability of factors of production at a given technology to decide on the optimal output. A manufacturing firm in the short run will keep on increasing various combinations of variable inputs till the marginal product (MP) equals average product. Once these two points converge, the MP will keep falling, bringing diminishing returns to the firm. The marginal product is the extra output produced by varying a single input or combination of inputs.

This neoclassical formulation cannot be applied as it is to media output because of its peculiar characteristics. Media output has intangible elements, which are the ideas and experiences that are valued by the consumer. Even though economic literature calls this the utility of the rational consumer and has an elaborate way of defining and measuring it, it is still complicated when applied to media products. These aspects are discussed further in the following section on media goods as hedonic goods. For newspapers and television channels, the average utility over a prolonged period is important. Since they are subscription-based products, they allow producers to manage demand over long time periods. So, determining how much to produce for products like newspapers and television channels is comparatively easy when compared to single-time demand products like films or pay-per-view services on television. The number of copies of a film that have to be made will depend on how audiences are expected to respond to it. Since this cumulative perception cannot be forecast, filmmakers focus on pre-release marketing, star value and front loading to realise value. More about front loading will be discussed in Chapter 7 on the film industry.

Production function for media firms in the first copy stage

If we divide media production into two stages, i.e., the first copy stage and the distribution stage, we can observe that in the first copy stage the emphasis is on quality, and in the second stage it is on quantity. The first copy is the most important stage of any mass-produced media product, be it a newspaper, TV programme, film or book. The production function in this stage is complicated because of the multiple inputs involved. Theoretically, at this stage, a media producer can vary the inputs to achieve the best possible quality. However, this quality cannot be measured by the media producer accurately. Even if a content firm varies its variable inputs in many different ways, it cannot not be assured of audience popularity. For instance, if the inputs of a film project, i.e., script-writers, artists and direction personnel, are re-combined in different ways, there is no guarantee that it will yield a more efficient product that can give better utility to the consumer. Even if a well-established author is signed for the next book project, a book publisher would still not know how the book could turn out and whether readers would appreciate it. At the first copy stage, especially media products with single-time use face a blind spot when it comes to demand. For products like newspapers, where demand is managed on a long-term basis, there is some possibility of measuring how much to produce since it is about both quality as well as quantity. For instance, a newspaper editor might need a certain number of reporters, photographers and illustrators to produce a newspaper edition. If the editor needs to know the optimum labour force to produce the best bulletin, then she has to experiment with various combinations of labour inputs. If the numbers of labour units are progressively increased, the amount of output produced increases initially with increasing marginal productivity. This stage is characterised by increasing marginal product and reducing marginal costs.

After a certain period, the increase in labour inputs will lead to diminishing marginal returns. This stage is characterised by decreasing marginal product and increasing marginal costs. At this stage, increase in productivity can be sustained only by increasing the fixed inputs as well. So, for given fixed inputs, the increase in variable inputs will initially produce increasing returns and later diminishing returns. In this case it is also assumed that labour units are standardised units with equal efficiency. This, however, does not provide a satisfactory explanation to the quality aspect of the media product, which is more important in the first copy stage.

Production function for media firms in the distribution stage

In the second stage, i.e. the distribution stage, the media output has clear cost advantages resulting in economies of scale, as discussed earlier. As the quantity of output produced increases, the marginal and average costs decrease, providing increasing returns to scale. The production function in this stage is simpler because of only one variable input. The input-output relationship in the distribution stage can be quantified and measured very easily compared to the first copy stage, which is complicated with quality parameters and multiple inputs. For instance, if we take the earlier example of the newspaper, its management can easily take a decision on how many copies of the newspaper have to be published, as they can measure at what stage the Marginal Physical Product (MPP) equals the Average Physical Product (APP). While in the same case, a newspaper editor will find it difficult to decide on the optimal workforce to produce a quality newspaper. That is because the factor-product relationship in the first copy stage is complicated, while it is fairly simpler in the distribution stage.

Measuring demand for media products

Demand is defined as the quantity of a good or service desired by the buyers at a given price. The demand for a good or service is affected by its price, price of substitutable goods, income and tastes. The law of demand states that, other things being equal, quantity demanded and the price of the commodity are inversely related. It means that if the price of the good increases, the demand decreases, and if the price of the good decreases, the demand increases. Applying neoclassical economic laws to media goods poses many problems because of (a) the hedonic nature of media goods, and (b) media firms operate in dual product markets. Behavioural economics seems to offer better explanations for the demand for media goods.

Media goods as hedonic goods

Media goods are consumed not just for their utilitarian value but also for their symbolic value. Media goods are considered by some economists as *hedonic goods* or experience goods because they involve multisensory, fantasy and emotive aspects (Clement et al. 2006, 155). When people are required to make decisions regarding consuming hedonic goods which provide experiential enjoyment, they tend to compare them with utilitarian goods which offer practical functionality. Behavioural economists point out that even though the prospect of a hedonic purchase is appealing to consumers, they find it very difficult to justify because of the guilt associated with consuming a non-utilitarian good. This is attributed to a culture that values hard work and parsimony. The chances of consuming a hedonic good seem to increase if consumers are in a position to justify the consumption. Bundling the purchase of hedonic good with a promised contribution to charity, or receiving it as a gift, seems to reduce the guilt associated with consuming hedonic goods (Strahilevitz and Myers 1998, 435).

When consumers are given a choice between paying money and spending time in exchange for acquiring different goods, consumers show a relative preference to pay in money for utilitarian purchases (shoulds) and in time for hedonic purchases (wants) (Okada 2005, 51). When people try to justify their expenditures on media products, it seems to be easier to justify time expenditures than money expenditures. For consumers in general, probably the opportunity cost of money is relatively easier to assess than the opportunity cost of time. However, this might vary with income levels.

Hedonic goods are characterised by their uniqueness, seasonality, information asymmetry and other subjective quality attributes like emotion that are very hard to measure. These characteristics result in short lifecycles and rapidly declining demand curves for media goods. Consumers of certain types of media goods also tend to make impulsive and highly subjective decisions as they involve low cognitive involvement and high emotional involvement. Clement suggests that three types of factors affect demand for hedonic goods—environmental factors, product-specific factors and adopter-specific factors (Clement 2006, 158). Environmental factors include competition, marketing, seasonality, and piracy. Product-specific factors include star power, director, lyricist, singer and music director. Adopter-specific factors include demographics, psychographics, and peer groups. A media firm generally focuses on product-specific factors first. But to increase demand for their products, they should try to influence environmental and adopter-specific factors. For instance, a film's financial success will depend not only on its product features, but also on environmental conditions like promotion and adopter-specific factors such as consumer's need to justify consumption and the cultural need to be accepted by peers.

Demand for goods in dual product markets

Demand forecasting measures work well for products whose price is paid by the final consumer or user. If the price of the good or service is subsidised by a third party either fully or partially, then it affects the measurement of demand. Many non-price determinants of demand come into play in such circumstances. Most media products, including newspapers, radio and TV shows and online portals, are supported by advertisers. The demand for media products is determined by both the end users and the advertisers who want access to those audiences. If the advertisers' demand for audience access reduces, the consumers should be willing to fill the gap, otherwise the supply of media products will be affected. In the case of European markets, the newspaper publishers are caught in a vicious cycle where falling readership means reduced support from the advertisers. When the advertiser support falls, the media firm will be forced to shift this cost to the consumer, who is not willing to pay the increased price, leading to a further fall in demand.

The demand for access to audiences plays a significant role in determining the supply of media products. However, it varies for different media products. Demand for access to audiences is very crucial in the case of newspapers, while it is less crucial in the case of films. For instance, an issue of an established English newspaper daily in India is priced at INR 5.00, while it might cost between INR 15 and INR 20 per copy, depending on the circulation. In this case the strategy of the newspaper firm is to forego a part of the subscription revenues, so that it can increase its circulation and readership. The lost subscription revenues are recovered from the advertising market. Significant demand for newspapers is in the form of monthly subscriptions, while a small portion comes from stand sales and hawkers. This low pricing strategy helps the newspaper publishers manage demand through monthly subscriptions. If the newspapers are sold at INR 15, the utility might still be the same for users, but the willingness of the consumer to pay will come down drastically as they will not be able to justify the spend. It will be impossible to achieve the circulation and readership they enjoy at lesser prices.

Some services like cable are available only on a monthly subscription basis. This allows for better demand management. For magazines, the demand is equally shared between subscriptions and stand sales. Almost all radio broadcasts and most television broadcasters are free to air, while a few premium entertainment channels charge subscription fees. Books and films are the only media products for which the price is almost fully paid by consumers.

Time allocation and demand for media products

Across the world consumers spend some time on media, even when they do not spend money. Some minimal level of time spent on media may be a non-discretionary necessity, much like eating, resting, washing, etc. If this is so, then the consumer within our existing social structure cannot choose to exclude media; her discretion is to choose among those media and vehicles with which she prefers to spend time (Hornik and Schlinger 1981, 351). Media consumers pay both monetarily and with time for media products. National average of time spent on media per day has gradually increased over the years (Kohli-Khandekar 2010, xviii). Time allocation by consumers can probably provide interesting insights into increasing media consumption.

Time allocation by media consumers can be used as a proxy for measuring the demand for media products. Time allocations by consumers are mostly monetised through advertising revenues. Measuring media product demand solely based on the price will not reveal a clear picture of demand. Time allocation metrics available in the market are not comprehensive and have severe deficiencies. As the time allocation by consumers is shifting in favour of convergent media devices like desktops, laptops and mobile devices, the allocations of advertising spends also change. Though time allocation by consumers is increasing rapidly, advertising allocations are not increasing commensurately with it, leaving a monetisation gap in some sub-segments of media. Such situations arise in the short run, but they get adjusted with time. Various structural factors hold back advertisers from shifting quickly to the new media favoured by consumers.

Time is required to consume media products. Media goods are plenty and abundant at any given point of time, but the consumer's time to consume them is limited. Consumers can choose either to fully utilise free time for recreational purposes, or to use some of this time to generate additional income (Vogel 2001, 10). This makes time a very valuable commodity in the context of consuming media products. Value is not destroyed in the process of media consumption but is produced in the form of advertising revenue. This has led some segments of the media industry to develop their revenue models based on consumer time, especially broadcasting. Depending on their intensity of engagement with various forms of media, consumers allocate money and time for a variety of media products. For media products where consumer engagement intensity is light, they are likely to spend their time, and where the engagement intensity is high, they are likely to spend money. A media consumer substitutes money with time depending on the value she attaches to the utility of the media products consumed. Demand forecasting in the case of media products has to take into account all these peculiar conditions.

Media product pricing

Pricing is the process of determining the monetary value in exchange for a unit of good or service. In the case of media products, their utility to consumers cannot be neatly translated into price. Utility is a weaker measure for determining price in this context. Even though costs are important in determining prices, many other factors like quality, competition, brand and other environmental factors too play an important role in determining price. Since most of the media firms operate in the dual product markets, their pricing strategies have to consider both the content markets and the advertising markets. The pricing strategies that will be followed by a media firm that will operate only in either content market or advertising market will have to be different from the media firms that will operate in both markets.

Pricing in content markets

Media firms which operate only in content markets are very few. Books, music albums, films, home video and some broadcast content firms operate purely in content markets. While all the earlier firms work in retail content markets, the last one works in Business to Business (B2B) content markets.

In retail content markets, pricing strategies have to ensure that costs are recovered from the end consumer and hence they tend to price in the cost plus mode. Cost plus is a pricing strategy in which the selling price is arrived at by adding profit margin to the product's unit cost. Cost plus pricing is justified from the producers' perspective but cannot be justified from the consumer perspective. This forces media firms operating only in the content markets to consider various other factors while pricing. Publishers follow premium pricing or high margin strategy while publishing non-fiction works in small quantities, e.g., coffee table books. High-priced academic books are published in hardback, and the costs are realised through institutional and library sales. Publishers follow a low-margin, high-volume pricing strategy while dealing with popular fiction works. If a star author is signed, and if there are few or no close substitutes in that genre during the period of release, then the publisher will have greater leeway in making the pricing decision. However firms operating only in content markets cannot go beyond a level in price competition, as it affects them collectively.

Product differentiation is a more preferred mode of competition than price competition among firms in content markets. Media firms use block pricing strategy in content markets. For instance, home video firms and music recording companies come up with product bundling strategies like compilation albums and DVD packs, forcing consumers to make an all-or-none decision. This is seen as the best way to extract residual market value besides reducing costs related to producing, distributing and marketing them as single units.

In B2B content markets, pricing strategies differ as there are few players. Broadcast content that can deliver higher Television Ratings (TVRs) can command premium pricing; the rest have to struggle for recognition in the market. Broadcast rights for popular sports are sold through a bidding process. This has led to astronomical prices due to cutthroat competition among broadcasters to acquire rights for sporting events. These high costs are transferred to the distributors and end consumers. But other forms of broadcast content do not enjoy such demand and pricing options.

Pricing in advertising markets

Not many media firms operate purely in advertising markets either. Free newspapers and free-to-air broadcasters operate only in advertising markets. Pricing in advertising markets is very well codified compared to pricing in content markets. A variety of services provided by audience measurement companies provides the basis for decision making in advertising markets (discussed in detail in Chapter 4). Purchase decisions in advertising markets are taken well in advance, and commitments are made in bulk. Various comparative measures like CPM (cost per thousand impressions), CPC (cost per click) and CPA (cost per acquisition) are available for buyers to evaluate comparative media prices. Peak load pricing strategy is followed in broadcast advertising markets. Since most of the advertisers want spots during prime time, broadcasters price these slots at a higher rate.

Pricing in dual markets

Many media firms are exposed to both content markets and advertising markets simultaneously. Newspapers and broadcasters are important examples of firms operating in both these markets. The ratio of revenues from both these markets differs among various media firms. Films are significantly exposed to content markets in their initial box office and home video phases, but eventually they get exposed to advertising markets when they enter broadcast windows. Within the broadcast window, a film might go through both the pay mode and the advertising mode. The pay mode pricing strategy can be on-demand pricing or access-based pricing.

In the cases of media output operating in dual markets, the output has to be made to suit the advertiser's interests as well. The advertiser might be interested in a certain demographic profile, psychographic profile or income profile. The value to the consumer based on the cover price and the value to the advertiser based on the consumer profile are interconnected and cannot be neatly distinguished in dual markets. This throws up dilemmas in pricing. If a newspaper has to increase its cover price to increase revenues, it will be worried about its effect on circulation and therefore on advertising revenues.

This chapter provided a comprehensive understanding of revenue streams and cost structures in media industries, besides issues related to how much to produce, how to measure demand and how to price media products. In the process, it also introduced concepts including Baumol's cost disease, clustering in media industries, media as hedonic goods and time allocation and demand for media products.

References

Arrese, A. (2006). Issues in media product management. In A. B. Albarran, S. M. Chan-Olmsted, and M. O. Wirth (Eds.), *Handbook of Media Management and Economics*. New York: Routledge.

Clement, M., Fabel, S., and Schmidt-Stolting, C. (2006). Diffusion of hedonic goods: A literature review. *International Journal on Media Management*, 8(4), 155–163.

Davidson, C. (2009). Dubai: Foreclosure of a dream. *Middle East Report*, 251, 8–13. Retrieved from www.jstor.org/stable/27735295

Doyle, G. (2002). *Understanding Media Economics*. London: Sage Publications.

Hornik, J., and Schlinger, M. J. (1981). Allocation of time to the mass media. *Journal of Consumer Research*, 7(4), 343–355.

Karlsson, C., and Picard, R. G. (2011). Media clusters: What makes them unique? In C. Karlsson and R. G. Picard (Eds.), *Media Clusters: Spatial Agglomeration and Content Capabilities*. Cheltenham, UK: Edward Elgar Publishing.

Kind, H., Nilssen, T., and Sørgard, L. (2009). Business models for media firms: Does competition matter for how they raise revenue? *Marketing Science*, 28(6), 1112–1128. Retrieved from www.jstor.org/stable/23884300

Kohli-Khandekar, V. (2010). *The Indian Media Business* (Third Ed.). New Delhi: Sage Publications.

KPMG. (2019). Indian media and entertainment report. India's digital future: Mass of niches. Retrieved September 16, 2020, from https://assets.kpmg/content/dam/kpmg/in/pdf/2019/08/india-media-entertainment-report-2019.pdf

Lorenzen, M., and Mudambi, R. (2010). Bangalore vs. Bollywood: Connectivity and catch-up in emerging market economies. *Academy of International Business Insights*, 10(1), 7–11.

Minasian, J. R. (1964). Television pricing and the theory of public goods. *Journal of Law and Economics*, 7, 71–80.

Okada, E. M. (2005). Justification effects on consumer choice of hedonic and utilitarian goods. *Journal of Marketing Research*, 42(1), 43–53.

Preston, P., and Sparviero, S. (2009). Creative inputs as the cause of Baumol's cost disease: The example of media services. *Journal of Media Economics*, 22(4), 239–252.

Strahilevitz, M., and Myers, J. (1998). Donations to charity as purchase incentives: How well they work may depend on what you are trying to sell. *Journal of Consumer Research*, 24(4), 434–446. Retrieved from www.jstor.org/stable/10.1086/209519

Vogel, H. (2001). *Entertainment Industry Economics: A Guide for Financial Analysis*. Cambridge, UK: Cambridge University Press.

3

AUDIENCES AND ADVERTISING MARKETS

Dual product markets: interplay *of audiences, advertising* and *media*

Most of the media products operate in dual product markets (discussed in Chapter 1). Content markets provide subscription revenues, while audience markets provide advertising revenues to the media firms. Audience markets are where the advertisers interact with the media firms. In audience markets, media firms compete to aggregate audiences and trade them with the advertisers for advertising spends. Advertising activity connects the media economy with the overall economy. This also explains why the media economy is more vulnerable to changes in the economy compared to other sectors. When the economy grows, the media sector growth rate is much higher than the overall economy, and when the economy shrinks, it falls much faster than the overall economy. In this chapter, we will examine how long-term changes in audience markets and advertising markets affect the chances of media firms to survive, grow and prosper besides audience measurement systems. The stage of a given media subsector in the lifecycle of the industry affects the ability of firms in that sector to attract consumer spends and advertising spends. For instance, consumer spends on digital media are expected to slow down in the next few years, while advertising spends are projected to increase. Shifts in consumer spends and advertising spends at the macro level can impact the business models of the firms and can also alter the market structures in the media industry.

Impact of consumer spends on media industry

Global consumer spending on media was estimated at US $1.14 trillion in 2015, and it is projected to reach US $1.45 trillion in 2020. Consumer spends are

DOI: 10.4324/9781003199212-3

spread over electronic devices, access charges, content purchases and rentals. Video games and broadband segments with projected CAGR of 9.1% and 7% respectively are far ahead of newspapers and consumer magazines with CAGR of −0.8% and −2.8% respectively (McKinsey's Global Media Report 2016). Consumers are also shifting their spending preferences with the maturation of digital media access and device penetration. Once the access and devices are ready, users should be willing to spend on content. Over the last few years, consumers are showing less interest in owning content and preferring access instead. Since the cost of accessing content is lower than the cost of owning it, overall revenues from content for media firms may dip in the short run. However, the lower cost of access will encourage more people to access paid services and discourage piracy, thereby boosting the long-term revenues. The success of OTT video and audio streaming services in the last few years substantiate this proposition.

Principle of relative constancy and beyond

It has been empirically established that media firms perform well during the boom years because of increased advertising spends by corporations and increased media spends from audiences. On the contrary, during recession, they face a double squeeze on their revenues as both consumers and advertisers cut back on expenditures. In this section, we will examine the impact of consumer spends on the performance of media firms.

The principle of relative constancy, or constancy hypothesis, is a model suggested by Maxwell E. McCombs, expanding on the earlier work of Charles E. Scripps. It helps in providing a macro-level explanation of expenditures on media by consumers. This model suggests that media is a staple in modern economies like food, clothing, shelter or healthcare, and hence a relatively constant portion of GDP is spent on it every year. This means that when the GDP grows, the share of media spends also grows, and when the GDP growth is negative, media spends fall. The model assumes that only a general expansion of the economy can infuse more money into the media industry. Since overall media spend as percentage of GDP has a ceiling in this model, media sub-segments like films, music, radio, TV and digital media can grow only by taking away the share of others, when the GDP is constant. Some gain, so others must lose, because no new money is diverted from the other sectors of the economy (McCombs 1972, 6). McCombs gives the example of how the income from movie admissions went to a peak in 1946 in the United States and from then on went into a steady decline for decades. These were also the years during which television increasingly saturated American households. During this period of decline for movie admissions, the overall media spends as percentage of GDP have remained constant, while spends on television grew exponentially.

This hypothesis also suggests that a household's budgets maintain a fixed portion of the available income for communication and entertainment products. Since the consumer budget allocation as a portion of their income is constant, they cannot buy all the available media products. They have to prioritise a media-mix over a range of media products that meet the same function. McCombs states that the money to create both radio and television seems to have come more from changing media habits and general economic growth than from any fundamental shifts in consumer habits—such as allocating mass media a larger share of personal income (McCombs 1972, 18–19). McCombs looked at long-term trends to suggest that advertiser spending on media and consumer spending on media is almost constant across media sub-segments. He observes that the ever-increasing media mix available to consumers and advertisers has not altered the constancy.

This model also suggests that arrival of new media technologies cannot alter the constancy. McCombs demonstrated this by examining the consumer spends on American television during the years 1949–1959, a period of significant economic growth in America. His study found that the constancy remained, while the spends on television grew rapidly. Despite the arrival of new technology, the overall spends on media have stayed the same as a percentage of GNP during this period. According to McCombs, the increased spends on television came along with the increase in incomes during this period and from re-allocations from radio and movies. The new technology, however, did not manage to get non-media spends to be diverted to media. This proposition places huge economic constraint on new technologies in the media industry. The older media will be affected by the arrival of new media technologies, and they will go through decline and restructuring. As new technologies come, older media products and the organisational forms also go through changes.

Many empirical studies were conducted to verify the constancy hypothesis after it was proposed by McCombs in his article "Mass Media in the Market Place." Some studies affirmed the hypothesis, while some pointed out aberrations to it. McCombs conducted a cross lagged correlational analysis to demonstrate the relationship between GNP and total consumer spending on mass media in the United States. Later PRC studies (cited in Lacy and Noh 1997, 4) examine aberrations to the PRC. They demonstrate that the introduction of VCR technology in the 1980s increased media spends as percentage of GDP. A study by Michel Dupagne in the Belgian context suggests that price and population are better variables to predict media expenditures than income, as suggested by the PRC model (Lacy and Noh 1997, 5). This study strengthened the criticism that PRC suffers from economic determinism, as it suggests that economic wealth alone is the determinant of media expenditures.

PRC also assumes that media sub-segments are in direct competition with one another, while they also complement each other in many ways. In the case of the VCR, it functions more as a complement to movies and television than as a competitor; PRC ignores such nuances. McCombs himself maintains that the accuracy of the PRC will be somewhat diminished when advertising expenditures alone are considered (McCombs 1972, 30). Heavily advertiser-supported media cannot be explained by PRC. For instance, in the Indian context, newspapers get almost 75–80% of their incomes from advertisers, while around only 20–25% come from subscriptions. In such cases, PRC fails to explain the phenomenon adequately, as advertising is a bigger determinant than income.

The new media technologies are also blurring the boundaries of media and non-media products. In the hybridised environment, such clear distinctions do not seem to be tenable. McCombs's hypothesis of economic constraints on mass media is based primarily on consumer incomes. Income constrains buying in all cases, and it is not something that specifically afflicts media spends. The PRC ignores the aspect of time. As new media technologies kept expanding, growing, and evolving, the amount of time spent by consumers on media per se has been gradually increasing. This was also enabled by increasing mechanisation and digitisation that increased leisure time. Even though they are not paying directly, they have been paying attention to media. The cost of time can explain many missing links in PRC even though measuring it would be very difficult.

PRC is critiqued for failing to consider earlier economic theories and concepts like demand, utility and opportunity costs, while proposing the hypothesis. This, according to them, has resulted in proposing simple and elegant explanations on consumer spending, and on media competition (Lacy and Noh 1997, 12).

Impact of advertising spends on media industry

Global advertising spending was estimated at $451 billion in 2015, and it was projected to increase to $602 billion by 2020. In 2015, television was ahead of all other sub-sectors of media in attracting advertising spend. Television received 40% of total advertising spend worldwide in 2015, followed by digital at 27% and print at 13% (McKinsey's Global Media Report 2016). McKinsey's Global Media Report predicts that digital spending, which grew by 17.5% in 2015, will account for more than 45% of overall media spend by 2020. The rapid expansion of fixed broadband and mobile broadband is seen as the prime driver of digital spends. Within digital media, mobile segment is attracting advertising spends and growing at a faster rate. This rapid digital shift is expected to have a structural effect on all media sub-sectors, forcing them to redefine their business models (McKinsey's Global Media Report 2015, 13).

Advertising activity has a significant impact on the financial performance of media firms. Advertiser interest in certain demographic and psychographic profiles is made adequately clear to content producers. This affects the behaviour of media firms to an extent that they focus on producing content that will be able to attract such audiences. Firms which are able to attract the desired audience profile will be able to attract more advertising spends. In media sub-sectors where advertising revenues are significant, their content will be primarily aimed at attracting the audience profile which advertisers are interested in. Advertising activity converts audience into a product that can be traded based on attention. There are economists who opine that audience is the main product of media and not content (Smythe 1981, 26). However, the nature of audience product is different from media product. Unlike media content, which has virtually unlimited shelf life and can be sold and resold indefinitely, the shelf life of media audiences is exceptionally short, lasting only for the period in which a media product is consumed (Napoli 2003, 30). The perishable nature of the audience product puts it in league with airlines, railways and roadways, where inventory management is crucial. Once the new issue of a daily newspaper arrives, or once a radio or TV broadcast is complete, the potential audience is lost forever. This makes it imperative for the media firms to sell their audience product even before it is accessed. Napoli explains this phenomenon by dividing audience product into three components—predicted audience, measured audience and actual audience. Predicted audience, the first component of the audience product, is used by media firms to enter into contracts. The second component, measured audience data, is used to verify the predicted audience. It becomes the final currency for settling the original transaction which was based on estimates. The greater the congruence between the predicted audience and the measured audience, the more efficient the transaction (Napoli 2003, 31). The measured audience becomes the predicted audience for the next set of transactions. The measured audience is the statistical representation of the actual audience, but never the actual audience. If the measured product does not reflect the actual audience adequately, the value of the audience product gets undermined among its stakeholders. As long as the quality of audience measurement is accepted by the advertisers, the media sub-sector in question will enjoy advertiser support. When the audience product loses credibility, the sub-sector will see desertion by advertisers and will be forced to look for alternate revenue streams to sustain.

Audience data is fundamental for media firms that depend completely on advertising revenues. Apart from the advertisers, even the investor community will be interested in the audience product. In the absence of other parameters, audience data will be a useful proxy for making investments in media firms as it gives some idea about the potential advertising revenues and thereby the financial performance of the firms. Even in equity markets, the stock prices of media firms with better audience measurement figures fare better.

Changes in advertising spends have a larger impact on the financial performance of media firms compared to consumer spends. This is because consumer spends are distributed over device purchases, access charges and subscription charges. Whenever new technologies arrive in the market, consumers have to invest on devices and access charges, which leave them with fewer resources to spend on content. Consumer spends are distributed over electronics manufacturers, telecom service providers and ISPs besides content. Whereas, advertising spends are spent only to get consumer attention. Another important factor is that consumer spends are small in size and are distributed over millions of consumers, whereas advertiser spends are concentrated in the hands of hundreds and in some case thousands. The volume of advertiser spends gives them better leverage over media firms and the content they produce in comparison to consumers. With a series of mergers and acquisitions in the last few decades, the big four of advertising—Omnicom, Interpublic, WPP and Publicis—have come to control 50% of advertising spends globally. With such huge resources, the fate of media sectors and firms is decided by the actions of advertising firms. The role of advertising activity on the performance of media firms increases further during the recession years. This happens because consumers reduce their spends on media but relatively, spending by corporations continue as they have to sustain their brands. Big brands prefer to spend during a recession as it gives them better visibility due to there being less clutter.

Media audience measurement—an introduction

Audience research and measurement can be defined as the specialised branch of media research dedicated to quantifying (size) and qualifying (characteristics) media audiences/viewers. In a media-saturated world, where a wide range of media is available for advertising, a rating mechanism is required for advertisers to decide on the reach and efficacy of their campaigns. For instance, if it is print media, advertisers use the circulation figures given by Indian Readership Survey for making advertising decisions. In the case of television, advertisers and media planners depend on Television Rating Points (GRPs or TRPs) for making these decisions. Ratings services are available in many media sub-sectors, including radio and digital media. To put it simply in the advertising markets worth billions of rupees, decisions are taken based on the audience metrics produced by audience measurement service providers.

Users of audience metrics and its uses

Advertisers, ad agencies, media planners, media buying agencies, publishers and broadcasters all use audience metrics. They subscribe to the various rating services and reports provided by the audience metrics companies. These reports are then used to devise their respective content and marketing strategies.

Major advertisers in India like HUL, Procter & Gamble, Tata Group, Aditya Birla Group, Hero Group, Dabur, Britannia, etc., will be very interested in knowing the returns they are getting from advertising in different media. For instance, decisions regarding whether to advertise on a TV channel, on which programme to air the ad and at what time it should be aired and in what frequency are taken based on the channel or programme ratings, and related information: the audience income, geography, language, gender, age, etc.

Ad agencies and media planners use audience metrics for suggesting to their clients the effective media plan for various media. The suggestions will be based on the ratings, class of audience and their lifestyles. For instance, if a car company wants to advertise for their latest premium category car, then the media planners will suggest channels that give them SEC A+ (Socio Economic Classification) or SEC A audiences, who will be their prime target. The advertising agencies also use the ratings data to calculate cost-per-thousand (CPM), which refers to the cost incurred to reach 1,000 members of the target audience, and cost-per-rating point (CRP), which refers to the cost incurred on each rating point. This will help the advertising agencies compare the effectiveness of the ad spend with competitors in the same media and with other media.

Newspapers, broadcasters and other advertiser-supported content producers use ratings data for continuously monitoring their reach and audience shares and to assess how they are faring with the competition. The data will be useful for the content staff to evaluate their content performance, plan for new content and reposition the existing content. Publishers and broadcasters use the ratings data to sell airtime. Tariff cards and airtime packages are prepared based on the ratings.

Audience metrics in India

Audience metrics began in India with the formation of Audit Bureau of Circulations (ABC) in 1948. Major newspaper publishers, advertising agencies and advertisers came together to form this initiative on the lines of ABC in the United States, which was formed in 1914. Twice a year, ABC would audit and certify the circulations of their member publications. These statistics work as an assurance to the advertisers on circulation. However, these are only circulation figures and do not provide details of readership, which advertisers are interested in. The first National Readership Survey in India (NRS) was conducted in 1970 by Operations Research Group (ORG). Its methodology was disputed by some stakeholders. But newspapers used this data to extensively promote themselves among advertisers and advertising agencies (Jeffrey 1994). NRS-II was done in 1978 and NRS-III in 1984; by then the service had received acceptance from all the important stakeholders despite the deficiencies in measuring process. NRS-IV was conducted in 1990, and the important feature was collection of information related to income and expenditure that helps in classification of audiences (Jeffrey 1994, 756–762). NRS is conducted by the National Readership Survey Council, formed with members from Indian Newspaper Society (INS), Advertising Agencies Association of India (AAAI), and Audit Bureau of Circulations (ABC). Indian Readership Survey (IRS) was launched in 1995 by Media Research Users Council (MRUC), as some of the stakeholders were unhappy with NRS. The competing ratings services were a cause of concern for advertisers and ad agencies because they came up with different samples and different reports, which were conflicting. NRS was discontinued in 2006. After protracted negotiations for years the governing bodies of both ratings agencies agreed to merge them into one in 2009. The new entity, Research Studies Council of India (RSCI), has been conducting the unified ratings service IRS from 2010. Similarly competing ratings services in television, Television Audience Measurement (TAM) and Indian National Television Audience Measurement (INTAM), were merged in 2002 under pressure from users. Further TAM ratings were discontinued in 2015, when TAM merged with Broadcast Audience Research Council (BARC

India), giving way to BARC ratings. The reasons for market participants discouraging competition in ratings markets will be discussed later in the chapter.

Audience measurement systems and issues

There are a lot of issues and problems related to the audience metrics. We will discuss some of the important problems faced by the ratings industry and user industry currently.

Measuring methodology

Many issues related to the measuring methodology of the ratings companies are being raised. Ratings service providers use surveys, diaries, audimeters, people meters, etc., to measure readership, listenership and viewership. Each of these methodologies has their own flaws, as they require audience involvement at various levels. For instance, when a person in the sample household watching a broadcast programme leaves the room (e.g. to answer a phone call) and forgets to release the button on the people meter, it produces wrong viewership figures on extrapolation. If a viewer sitting before the television set gets bored of the programme and tries reading something without switching off the TV set, even this time it will be counted for ratings. In 2014, 18 leading publishers across languages condemned IRS 2013 for flawed research. For instance, according to IRS 2013, Hindu Business Line has thrice as many readers in Manipur as in Chennai. Such anomalies create a trust deficit among stakeholders, as they clearly point to the divergence between measured audience and actual audience.

Sample size and representativeness

The most serious problem with audience metrics is their representativeness. The sample households both in terms of quality and quantity are often too few to be representative of the universe. For instance, for approximately 20,000 publications with 45 crore circulation in India, IRS 2018 survey had 3.6 lakh respondents across 91 individual districts and 101 district clusters. BARC, the leading TV ratings service provider in the country, has a sample size of 44,000 meters for approximately 200 million TV households in 2020.

New technologies and audience fragmentation

Historically, changes in media technologies and audience measurement technologies have had significant impact on audience markets. Advancements in media technologies have fragmented the audiences by increasing distribution platforms. For instance, the television broadcast market, which used to be terrestrial, is fragmented into terrestrial, cable and satellite, DTH, IPTV, Mobile TV, OTT, VOD, etc. Technologies like personal digital video recorders allow viewers to record their shows without advertisements. The advertising industry and advertisers are very unhappy with fragmentation and with technologies that affect the engagement quality of their media vehicle. Capturing metrics data across multiple points of usage and integrating it to make it a valuable product to advertisers is not an easy task for measurement companies, as they do not have access to data on proprietary platforms. Measurement companies have to partner with such firms in the absence of legal provisions for compulsory sharing of data.

Tampering and manipulation

There are issues of hyping data and forging reports by measurement companies. Measurement companies often focus on large urban markets with concentrated audiences. Some measurement companies will also be obliged to do reporting in a way that suits their biggest subscribers. Further, there are issues related to trust. For instance, the information related to the sample people meter households for measuring TV viewers are supposed to be classified. If that information falls into the hands of the broadcasters, they will try to influence the sample households to increase their programme and channel ratings. More than once in the past few years, this information was leaked and was reported in business newspapers and TV channels. Such incidents raise some fundamental questions about trustworthiness of the ratings and makes the advertisers very sceptical.

Are audience metrics markets—natural monopolies?

The term *natural monopoly* is used to refer to a market situation where only one player is required. The users in these markets prefer the services of a monopolist to that of competition, to avoid some peculiar problems associated with competition in these markets. Even when these supposed natural monopolies are contested and in the ensuing slug between them, one shuts shop and the remaining one becomes a monopoly again. By nature, these kinds of markets prefer monopoly in the long run, even though competition happens in the short run. Even audience measurement services are identified by some economists as natural monopolies. Costs and convenience are reasons why market participants settle for monopoly metrics services even though they are imperfect. Competition is not preferred in these markets, as it increases transaction costs of participants and also destroys the idea of "accuracy," which is crucial for the currency status enjoyed by the metrics. Especially television markets worldwide are known for preferring monopoly services in metrics data. In the United States, Nielsen has been the de facto monopoly in national TV metrics markets. With its patents over the household Audimeter, Nielsen enjoyed a monopoly over measuring audience ratings for the network TV market for 30 years (Karen and Buzzard 2002, 274). Setting up a metrics service involves huge capital investment, technological expertise and, above all, creating an impression that they service is "reliable" and the service provider is "independent and autonomous." As discussed earlier in this chapter, the participants in advertising markets in India found competing data to be problematic and therefore preferred to avoid that situation by merging the competing services. Observing these tendencies, Philip Napoli opines that

> Audience marketplace illustrates two countervailing forces. On the one hand, the desire for better quality in audience measurement persists, because better measurement means higher quality of audience product. On the other hand, the audience marketplace wants a single parsimonious currency, something achievable only when the provider of audience data is a monopoly.
>
> *(Napoli 2003, 20–21)*

In a study conducted in the Indian context (Taneja 2013, 211–212), it was found that in fragmented markets, participants found innovative ways of using the services of the second audience measurement firm in the market. TAM was the de facto currency for making advertising decisions by market participants during the period 2002–2014, while the second service aMAP found favour with the broadcast networks. The broadcasters were using this service to do content monitoring, promotional planning and tactical scheduling. This happened because TAM updated its numbers weekly while aMAP issued its ratings daily, which made it more suitable for monitoring content performance by broadcasters. This example is used by Taneja to suggest that new players can find their own niche, since there are many interested parties who can sustain product differentiation in a fragmented media market. He further suggests that historically, new service providers in audience metrics markets had less niche overlap, resulting in destructive competition and return of monopoly condition.

The prevailing structure of deal making in Indian media markets between the agencies and broadcasters is for longer terms. Even if overnight data is made available, it does not help the market players, as they cannot modify purchasing decisions. Even the broadcaster's inventories will be sold out, especially the best ones, rendering the available data ineffectual.

The idea of a natural monopoly is not completely true. Some measurement companies also actively use proprietary technologies and user industry dilemmas to actively maintain monopoly status by warding off competition. The Harris Committee in the United States conducted hearings into Nielsen's monopoly in radio and TV measurement markets in the 1960s. The committee uncovered plans by Nielsen to dominate the market. The committee chastised Nielsen for acquiring competition through unfair means, using patent litigation for preventing entry of potential competitors, preventing competitors from developing competitive ratings and many such unfair practices to maintain its monopoly (Karen and Buzzard 2015, 515)

Future of audience markets

Advertisers are raising serious questions about the quality of the audience product produced by the measurement companies. Increasing media options has altered consumption patterns, and the resulting fragmentation of audiences is putting pressure on the audience measurement systems to upgrade. One of the important criticisms of media measurement systems has been its focus on media exposure, which measures the size and duration of exposure. Media exposure is only one dimension of media consumption, and probably an easily measurable one. Advertisers are interested to know other dimensions like engagement and product purchases, which are not captured in the existing measures. With the introduction of cost-per-action pricing models (CPA) in the digital markets, the traditional exposure-based cost-per-thousand (CPM) is facing resistance from advertisers. The rise of social media influencers in digital media spaces has given rise to influencer marketing. In these metrics one can know engagement rate besides impressions and the number of followers. Various measures including likes, retweets, shares, clicks, reactions and comments give a sense of engagement. However, the sales metrics of each influencer forms the bottom line.

Users are not happy with the extrapolation of the panel-based data and are increasingly looking at the possibility of developing a basket of currencies based on census data. Many attempts are being made to address these aspects. The industry is currently pushing for three screen approach, which includes measurement of TV, computer and mobile phone.

One of the new trends in media measurement worldwide is application of multiple data sources for measuring media usage. In these hybrid methods, data from survey research, panel-based measurement data and census data are analysed together. Sometimes by merging data from two or three different mono media surveys, valuable data can be produced. For example, print media data can be merged with television media data using some demographic or psychographic variables. This integrated approach attempts to leverage the best approaches in different methodologies to produce improved quality of data sets for media managers. Fused data is still not able to satisfy users to the extent they can use it as flawless currency. Advertisers and media planners wanting to have effective multimedia campaigns are driving this shift from mono media measurement to multimedia measurement systems. They want metrics comparable across media. The current mono media measuring systems cannot be compared with each other easily. The early survey-based methods both over telephone or in diary method used self-reporting and recall methods for tabulation media usage data. The respondents were chosen through sampling techniques. This has raised serious concerns about the accuracy and representativeness of these measures. The technology-based measurements that came later were also sample based. The samples were very small because the costs of increasing the sample were very high.

Media content on its debut gets lots of attention from the audience. A lot of expenditure on promotions is also a reason for this attention. But every media product has a very long life, where a smaller number of audiences continue to access it. Measuring the usage continuously even when the users trickle in is important, but it is not being done now. Media metrics agencies are yet to focus on this area. Single source might be a good way to measure the "short head," while the "long tail" needs various other measures. With increasing fragmentation and multiple accesses for the same content, the long tail of media is growing (Taneja and Mamoria 2012, 132). Data related to the long tail is also valuable as it continues to give revenues with almost no promotion costs.

Despite advancements in measuring methodologies, audience markets remain elusive and uncertain spaces. The very process of measuring audiences is at stake when the purchasers of audience product do not have any means of verifying whether what they have invested is worth the price. At some level, the whole audience marketplace seems to be operating on educated guesses and rule-of-thumb decisions, making it an unpredictable marketplace with uncertain products.

References

Jeffrey, R. (1994). Monitoring newspapers and understanding the Indian state. *Asian Survey, 34*(8), 748–763. doi:10.2307/2645262

Karen, S., and Buzzard, F. (2002). The peoplemeter wars: A case study of technological innovation and diffusion in the ratings industry. *Journal of Media Economics, 15*(4), 273–291. doi:10.1207/S15327736ME1504_4

Karen, S., and Buzzard, F. (2015). The rise of market information regimes and the historical development of audience ratings. *Historical Journal of Film, Radio and Television, 35*(3), 511–517. doi:10.1080/01439685.2015.1052219

Lacy, S., and Noh, G. (1997). Theory, economics, measurement and the principle of relative constancy. *Journal of Media Economics, 10*(3), 3–16.

McCombs, M. (1972, August). Mass media in the market place. *Journalism Monographs* (Vol.24). Association for Education in Journalism.

McKinsey's Global Media Report. (2015). Retrieved February 4, 2020, from https://www.mckinsey.com/~/media/McKinsey/dotcom/client_service/Media%20and%20Entertainment/PDFs/McKinsey%20Global%20Report%202015_UK_October_2015.ashx

McKinsey's Global Media Report. (2016). Retrieved February 4, 2020, from https://www.mckinsey.com/~/media/McKinsey/Industries/Technology%20Media%20and%20Telecommunications/Media%20and%20Entertainment/Our%20Insights/Global%20Media%20Report%202016/GMO%20Report_2016_Industry%20overview_v3.pdf

Napoli, P. M. (2003). *Media Economics: Media Institutions and the Audience Marketplace.* Cambridge: Cambridge University Press.

Smythe, D. W. (1981). *Dependency Road: Communications, Capitalism, Consciousness, and Canada.* Norwood, NJ: Ablex.

Taneja, H. (2013). Audience measurement and media fragmentation: Revisiting the monopoly question. *Journal of Media Economics, 26*(4), 203–219.

Taneja, H., and Mamoria, U. (2012). Measuring media views across platforms: Evolving audience information systems. *International Journal of Media Management, 14*(2), 121–140.

4

MEDIA ECONOMICS AND PUBLIC POLICY

Communications systems in democratic societies, including India, whether publicly or privately owned, present economic and political opportunities, which are sometimes at odds with one another. McChesney and Schiller (2003) capture the essential contradiction in these functions as a "vital tension," noting that, "The dual life of the communication system, at once a pivot of the emerging global economy and a key foundation of political democracy, constitutes a vital tension on the world stage" (p. 1). We see this vital tension in the opposing economic and regulatory forces that shape media industries. Since media products show economies of scale, media corporations have an economic rationale for expanding their reach. On the other hand, governments are concerned about controlling market dominance and monopolies to preserve diversity and plurality of views, especially in democracies. Thus, while governments move to regulate media industries, the corporations in these industries support deregulation. Additionally, deep interconnections across national boundaries and economies further complicate these opposing forces, as Lunt and Livingstone (2012) observe: "Government control over markets, social life and culture is challenged by the perceived imperative to deregulate in order to open up markets and so maximise the benefits of globalisation" (p. 2).

In the presence of market deficiencies such as the abuse of market dominance, the presence of externalities and information asymmetries in media markets, government policy and regulation attempt to provide solutions to prevent market failure. In this chapter we take a close look at media markets and the role played by governments.

Market deficiencies in media industries

We have learnt that media products have certain economic properties, i.e., they are public goods because they are non-rivalrous and non-excludable in their

DOI: 10.4324/9781003199212-4

consumption, they have a high first copy cost and their production shows increasing returns to scale. These properties create a strong economic incentive for media firms to expand their market share, with the result that media markets are prone to monopolistic dominance (Doyle 2002). In democracies, monopolistic and even oligopolistic media markets give cause for much concern since they have the potential to pose a threat to the cornerstone of any democracy—the opportunity for the expression of a plurality of political and social views. This is especially significant in a multiparty parliamentary democracy such as ours, which has extreme social, economic, linguistic and other types of diversity and which thrives on debate and the expression of a wide range of views.

Abuse of market dominance

Monopolies in some industries, such as landline telephony for instance, may be seen as beneficial because they can lead to enormous cost savings. We can imagine how expensive it would be if we had multiple companies laying landline cables to our homes, while we subscribed only to the one service. However, monopolies create the potential for abuse of market power by the dominant firm through raised prices because of the absence of strong enough competition to control prices. Second, there is a fear that in the absence of significant competition, the dominant firm will not have an incentive to introduce innovations which could increase product choice and quality. Third, through vertical and horizontal integration which are very attractive propositions for firms operating in industries with economies of scale, media firms could control access to audiences and therefore reduce opportunities for dissenting voices and pluralistic expression.

Monopolistic markets have thus been seen to require government intervention to rectify these market deficiencies. For instance, when utilities are delivered by monopolistic private corporations, such as in electricity or landline telephony, governments set price ceilings to prevent the abuse of market dominance.

Presence of externalities

A second area of market deficiency is the presence of externalities in media industries (Doyle 2002). It is possible that media products may have desirable or undesirable effects on society. Thus, while documentaries or other types of artistic media content may contribute to the education of the audience, this type of content may not be profit-making and thus optimum quantities of such content may not be produced by the firms in the market. As a society we might want to maximise the desirable effects—i.e., the positive externalities—and restrict the undesirable effects—i.e., the negative externalities.

Information asymmetry

Information asymmetry occurs when some players in the market have more information than other players. This difference can be exploited by oligopolistic firms colluding in cartels (Feinstein et al. 1985) to increase profits. The

Competition Commission of India observes that the presence of information asymmetry is an area of market deficiency that can cause "the invisible hand of the marketplace to malfunction" (Annual Report 2015).

In the following section, we examine some government interventions to rectify such market deficiencies.

Government interventions

Hendriks (1995) provides a handy framework to approach policies that affect media industries—policies that apply to all sectors of the economy (such as competition policy), policies that are specific to particular media industries (such as the press or broadcasting), and policies that are aimed at a particular media sector and affect other media sectors indirectly (such as policies towards television news which have an indirect effect on the newspaper industry). In this section we examine government interventions that restrain market power; encourage positive externalities through direct participation, production subsidies and import quotas; and reduce or prevent information asymmetries.

Restraint on market power

Restraints on market power typically take the form of market share and cross-ownership restrictions. From the earliest days of radio and television broadcasting in the United States, governments have acted to restrain the extent to which organisations could own radio and television stations in a particular market with the aim of ensuring plurality and diversity of voices in the media. Through the television *duopoly rule* and the *one-to-a-market rule*, the Federal Communications Commission (FCC), the US regulatory authority for communications industries, ensured that an organisation could only own one television station or radio station in a market (Singleton and Rockwell 2003).

Market power of media firms has been a matter of concern for over seven decades now, right from the early years of independent India. The First Press Commission in 1954 and the Second Press Commission in 1982 investigated print media ownership and noted the issue of concentration at the firm level (Nair 2003; Bhattacharjee and Agrawal 2018). From a market structure point of view, linguistic diversity in India is a key feature that needs to be considered while determining media markets (Nair and Taneja 2018; Chitrapu 2012). Based on languages and the states where they are spoken, India can be divided into 12 geographic markets; therefore, by using this framework, relevant media markets in India are defined by further taking into consideration the medium (e.g., television) and the genre (e.g., news) of the media product (TRAI 2014). The Telugu, Tamil and Malayalam language markets for daily newspapers, television news channels and television entertainment channels were all found to score high on measures of concentration with the presence of many conglomerate firms that were vertically and horizontally integrated with holdings in television, radio and print (ASCI 2009). The Competition Act (2002) was passed to place restraints on abuse of market power in many industrial sectors including media industries. We discuss this Act and some illustrative media cases before the Competition Commission of India at some length in a later section.

Controlling externalities

Internationally, government intervention to increase positive externalities has taken many forms including direct participation through public broadcasters, production subsidies and import quotas. The production and dissemination of audiovisual programming such as films and television programs in local languages is considered to have positive externalities by governments in Europe and Asia, as it plays a role in preserving local languages, culture and history.

Direct participation

Direct participation through public service broadcasters (PSBs) is one way in which governments intervene in markets that exhibit deficiencies, especially with regard to positive externalities. In Europe, 85 public service broadcasters belonging to an association called the European Broadcasting Union (EBU) were present in 56 countries with an average audience share of 28.8% in 2010 (Lewis 2012). These broadcasters include ARD and ZDF in Germany, RAI in Italy and France Télévisions in France. In India, the government plays a role in creating content that has positive externalities by direct participation in the terrestrial broadcasting sector through All India Radio (AIR) and the television network Doordarshan. Content for underserved demographics, such as farmers, for instance, is created through these entities. We discuss Doordarshan at greater length in Chapter 6 on television broadcasting.

Production subsidies

A second route is through extending production subsidies for content that is valued by governments that may not be produced at the optimum levels. Among others, subsidies to the film industry in countries such as France, Australia, China, Taiwan, Argentina, Chile, Bolivia and Peru have been documented in the research literature (see Jackel 2007; Gao 2009; Ross 2010; Parker and Parenta 2009). The French government levies a tax on film revenues at the box office as well as from broadcast and video sales called the "compte de soutiene" which is used to subsidise film makers. Additionally, the French government extends credit facilities, tax shelters and co-production support (Jackel 2007). The Chinese government provides film production subsidies as well as support to the exhibition sector in rural areas; similar support is offered by the Taiwanese government (Gao 2009).

Linguistic diversity is a key structural feature of Indian media markets, and through language-based production subsidies, Indian states support cinema in their native languages to varying degrees. The size and wealth of the linguistic population determines the total disposable income that may be spent on media products in that language (Waterman 1988; Wildman and Siwek 1988; Hoskins and Mirus 1988). Thus, media products in some Indian-language markets such as the Hindi, Tamil and Telugu markets receive greater economic support from audiences and have a higher output than do media products in markets where the language is spoken by fewer people, such as the Gujarati or Punjabi-language media markets (Chitrapu 2012). However, state governments see the production of media products such as films in their local languages as a desirable step towards preserving their languages and intervene through subsidies for such films (Chitrapu 2011). Films made in the state language also attract lower entertainment taxes than do films produced in other languages. In Maharashtra, the Entertainment Tax Refund Scheme in force till 1997 provided a refund of the entertainment tax collected on a Marathi-language film; when the producer made her next film, this was replaced by a full waiver on entertainment tax on all Marathi films from 1997 to 2000 when other aid mechanisms were instituted (Narwekar 1995). From 2006 onwards, Tamil-language films with Tamil-language titles were exempted from the 15% entertainment tax. From 2011, all Tamil films with a U-certificate from the censors were further examined by a state-appointed committee and could be exempted from entertainment tax, which in the meantime had doubled to 30% (Ravindranath 2017).

Import quotas

Some films and television programs are considered to have negative externalities in that they are seen as "a cultural invasion" promoting values and culture that are alien and undesirable and governments would like to restrict their exhibition in their countries. Quotas are thus a third route taken by governments that intervene in markets where negative externalities are perceived to be present. Asian countries including Japan and South Korea impose quotas on the import and screening of international films in a bid to preserve film production in their languages (Lee 2003; Lee and Bae 2004). Before Indian markets were liberalised in the 1990s, film imports in India had a particularly undesirable externality for a government that was on a path of self-sufficiency in response to colonialism. The import of films resulted in a drain of precious foreign exchange that the government was determined to avoid at any cost. Pendakur (1985) notes that in 1957, the Indian government entered into an agreement with the Motion Picture Export Association of America (MPEAA), an organisation consisting of the international distribution arms of eight Hollywood studios at that time, according to which only a certain number of films could be imported into India and only a certain amount of earnings could be repatriated, thereby conserving foreign exchange. Details of this agreement are to be found in the Report of the Working Group on National Film Policy published by the Ministry of Information and Broadcasting in 1980, and also known as the Karanth Committee report (Pendakur 1985).

Preventing information asymmetries

To prevent the abuse of information asymmetries and of market dominance, the government enacted the Competition Act (2002) and instituted the Competition Commission of India (CCI) which acts on complaints received from firms and investigates allegations of abuse of market power and awards cease-and-desist orders as well as monetary penalties. The Competition Act (2002) and the Competition (Amendment) Act (2007) were enacted to prevent anti-competitive practices, promote competition, safeguard consumer interests and promote free trade. Under the legal framework of this act, the Competition Commission of India (CCI) and the Competition Appellate Tribunal (COMPAT) were established in 2009.[1] The CCI functions under the purview of the Ministry of Corporate Affairs of the Government of India. Prior to the establishment of the CCI, anti-competitive practices were regulated by the Monopolies and Restrictive Trade Practices Commission (MRTPC) under the legal framework of the Monopolies and Restrictive Trade Practices Act (MRTP Act 1969), which was subsequently repealed in 2009.[2]

According to the CCI, the presence of information asymmetry and externalities cause the invisible hand of the marketplace to "malfunction."[3] Regulation is therefore required to prevent anti-competitive practices. Chapter II of the Competition Act contains four sections which deal with three main areas of anti-competitive behaviour—Section 3 deals with anti-competitive agreements, Section 4 deals with the abuse of dominant position and Sections 5 and 6 deal with combinations arising from mergers. The CCI thus regulates anti-competitive practices including price-fixing by cartels and unfair practices by dominant firms. This is done in order to maximise producers' as well as consumers' surplus and to promote the availability of greater choice as well as improvements in the quality of goods and services.[4] It also reviews mergers and acquisitions.[5] The CCI's deterrent to offending firms is through "cease and desist orders" and the imposition of sanctions (monetary penalties).[6]

From its very inception, the activities of media firms and industry bodies have been examined by the CCI based on complaints received from aggrieved firms. In the first six years (2009–2015) since its establishment in 2009, approximately 8% of all cases before the CCI cases pertained to the media industry (47 cases out of 586 cases). We look at some of these cases next.

FICCI-Multiplex vs UPDF

One of the earliest media industry cases before the CCI was *FICCI-Multiplex Association of India against United Producers Distributors Forum (UPDF) & others* (01/2009). The United Producers Distributors Forum was formed by members of existing film producers' associations in Mumbai who resolved to not release any Hindi films through multiplexes until their terms for revenue-sharing were met. This was held by the CCI to be in violation of section 3 of the Competition Act which prohibits anti-competitive agreements. The Commission ruled that multiplexes were consumers and their interest was threatened, and that the interest of the "common man," the final consumer of films, was also "adversely affected." Over two dozen members of the United Producers Distributors Forum were directed to refrain from such behaviour and were fined.

HT Media vs Super Cassettes

In the *HT Media Ltd. and M/s. Super Cassettes Industries Ltd.* (HT Media Limited v. Super Cassettes Industries Limited, 2014) case, Super Cassettes Industries Ltd (abbreviated as SCIL), one of the largest rights holders of Hindi film music, was reported to have charged excessively high fees for broadcast rights to its music and also imposed a minimum commitment charge regardless of the quantity of music played on radio stations including Fever 104, an FM radio station owned by HT Media. The Commission found that SCIL's actions limited consumers' access to music as well as limited other music companies' access to markets. It held that SCIL had violated section 4 (abuse of dominant position) of the Competition Act which prohibits a firm's abuse of its dominant position and imposed a fine of INR 2.83 crores on SCIL. SCIL was also ordered to modify the terms of its agreements with radio stations.

Ashtavinayak vs PVR

Film distributors' and exhibitors' associations have been successfully challenged by individual producers for violations of sections 3 (anti-competitive agreements) and 4 (abuse of dominant position) of the Competition Act, and penalties have been imposed on these associations in multiple cases before the CCI. An example is the case of *M/s Shri Ashtavinayak Cine Vision Limited Against PVR Picture Limited and Others* (71/2011), which deals with the hurdles faced by Ashtavinayak, a producer, over the release of its film *Rockstar* due to the anti-competitive behaviour of the opposite parties which included exhibitors and distributors' trade associations. The Commission found that certain practices of a distributors' association (named as opposing party no 2 in this case), Northern India Motion Pictures Association (NIMPA), were anti-competitive because among other things, its bye-laws prohibited members from dealing with non-members, it required compulsory registration of films that were to be released in its territory and it demanded holdbacks on release of films in any other media.

In the next section we examine the economic impact of government intervention in media markets.

Economic impact of government interventions

Governments directly and indirectly impact media industries through their interventions. As we know, media firms enjoy economies of scale and scope, i.e., the average cost per audience member falls as they reach larger audiences,. Additionally, through horizontal integration of media outlets, media firms are able to realise synergies in programming and cross-promotion (Albarran 2004).

Protectionist policies sometimes attract criticism for having effects that run counter to their aim. For instance, the imposition of import and screening quotas to prevent negative externalities in South Korea has been blamed for a deterioration in the quality of the films produced. It led to the production of "quota quickies"—poorly produced local films that were produced so that Korean film production houses could meet their domestic production quota and then import the more profitable Hollywood films (Lee 2003). The effect of this, as Lee (2003) notes, "actually hurt the development of the local film industry because film producers have less incentive to produce high quality films" (p. 117).

Media economics researchers point out that concentration in media industries has steadily increased (Albarran 2004). In the United States, the passage of the Telecommunications Act in 1996 (which allowed firms to own an unlimited number of television stations as long as the total households they reached was less than 35% of national television households) brought increased consolidation to the groups that owned television stations; the 210 groups present in 1995 were consolidated into 184 in 1997, i.e., a drop of 12.4%, with an increase in the number of stations owned by each group (Howard 1998).

In India, if we examine the government's role in regulating media content, carriage and trade, we find that it varies from sector to sector. Film content is directly regulated, with films requiring to be certified by the Central Board of Film Certification, a statutory body under the Ministry of Information and Broadcasting which works within the purview of the Cinematograph Act of 1952 (CBFC 2020). The content of broadcast radio and television is regulated by the broadcast wing of the Ministry of Information and Broadcasting in accordance with the Programme and Advertisement Codes of the Cable Television Networks (Regulation) Act, 1995 and the Cable Television Networks Rules, 1994. The broadcast television industry also self-regulates content through two industry bodies, the News Broadcasting Standards Authority and the Indian Broadcasting Foundation, which examine content-related complaints in news and entertainment, respectively. Print media content is not directly regulated. In terms of carriage, or distribution, television and radio broadcasting requires a government licence issued by the Ministry of Information and Broadcasting though the eligibility requirements do not pose high financial barriers to entry (Parthasarathi 2018). The Telecom Regulatory Authority of India (TRAI), a statutory body established by the Telecom Regulatory Authority of India Act, 1997 regulates tariffs, uplinking and downlinking, interconnection, addressable systems and quality of service of cable and satellite television in India. In terms of trade, in an earlier section we have discussed the role played by the Competition Commission of India to prevent anti-competitive practices.

Regulation vs deregulation

Regulation of media industries continues in many countries around the world in various forms with various intentions. Limits on Foreign Direct Investment in Indian media companies are an example of how the media industry in India is regulated. Content regulation in the film industry through the Central Board of Film Certification is another example of media industry regulation.

An increase in radio and television stations, as well as legal challenges from court cases that questioned the theoretical basis and efficiency of existing policies, provided the momentum to deregulation in American broadcasting from the 1970s onwards (Bates and Chambers 1999). The last two decades of the 20th century beginning with the Reagan presidency (1981–1988) in the United States, the passage of the Telecommunications Act in 1996 and other rulings, are identified as a period of widespread deregulation, a time when "the FCC took on a marketplace approach to regulation," leading to consolidation in many sectors of the American media industry and the creation of global media giants such as Vivendi Universal, Disney, Newscorp and Bertelsmann (Albarran 2004, p. 298). However, American media industry deregulation was also accompanied by challenges from critics who questioned the premise that "market forces would compel operation in the public interest" (Bates and Chambers 1999, 20).

Notes

1 Annual Report 2009–2010, Competition Commission of India.
2 Website of the Ministry of Corporate Affairs, Government of India.
3 Annual Report 2014–2015, Competition Commission of India.
4 Annual Report 2009–2010, Competition Commission of India (p. 1).
5 Annual Report 2009–2010, Competition Commission of India.
6 Annual Report 2014–2015, Competition Commission of India (p. 9).

References

Albarran, A. B. (2004). Media economics. In J. D. H. Downing, D. McQuail, P. Schlesinger, and E. Wartella (Eds.), *The SAGE Handbook of Media Studies* (pp. 291–308). London: Sage Publications.

Annual Report 2014–2015. (2015). Competition Commission of India. Retrieved from www.cci.gov.in/sites/default/files/annual%20reports/Annual%20Report%202014-15%20Eng.pdf

ASCI. (2009). *Study on Cross Media Ownership in India: Draft Report.* Hyderabad: Administrative Staff College of India.

Bates, B. J., and Chambers, T. (1999). The economic basis for radio deregulation. *Journal of Media Economics, 12*(1), 19–34.

Bhattacharjee, A., and Agrawal, A. (2018). Mapping the power of major media companies in India. *Economic and Political Weekly, 53*(29), 48–57.

CBFC. (2020). Central Board of Film Certification. Retrieved from www.cbfcindia.gov.in/main/about-us.html

Chitrapu, S. (2011, June). *The Political Economy of Indian Language Film Production: The Case of Marathi Cinema.* Paper presented at the Annual conference of the Asian Media Information and Communication Centre (AMIC), 24–27 June, Hyderabad, India.

Chitrapu, S. (2012). A regional mosaic: Linguistic diversity and India's film trade. In A. G. Roy (Ed.), *The Magic of Bollywood: At Home and Abroad* (pp. 81–106). New Delhi: Sage Publications.

Doyle, G. (2002). *Understanding Media Economics.* Thousand Oaks, CA: Sage Publications.

Feinstein, J. S., Block, M. K., and Nold, F. C. (1985). Asymmetric information and collusive behavior in auction markets. *The American Economic Review, 75*(3), 441–460.

FICCI-Multiplex Association of India v. United Producers/Distributors Forum (Case 01/2009). (2011). Competition Commission of India. Retrieved from www.cci.gov.in/sites/default/files/FICCIOrder260511_0.pdf

Gao, Z. (2009). Serving a stir-fry of market, culture and politics on globalisation and film policy in Greater China. *Policy Studies, 30*(4), 423–438.

Hendriks, P. (1995). Communications policy and industrial dynamics in media markets: Toward a theoretical framework for analyzing media industry organization. *Journal of Media Economics, 8*(2), 61–76.

Hoskins, C., and Mirus, R. (1988). Reasons for the US dominance of the international trade in television programmes. *Media, Culture, and Society, 10,* 499–515.

Howard, H. H. (1998). The 1996 telecommunications act and TV station ownership: 1 year later. *Journal of Media Economics, 11*(3), 21–32.

HT Media Limited v. Super Cassettes Industries Limited (Case 40/2011). (2014). Competition Commission of India. Retrieved from www.cci.gov.in/sites/default/files/C-2011-40_0.pdf

Jackel, A. (2007). The inter/nationalism of French film policy. *Modern & Contemporary France, 15*(1), 21–36.

Lee, B., and Bae, H.-S. (2004). The effect of screen quotas on the self-sufficiency ratio in recent domestic film markets. *Journal of Media Economics, 17*(3), 163–176.

Lee, S.-W. (2003). *Trading in Film: The Role of Government Regulation.* Korea Information Strategy Development Institute (KISDI).

Lewis, D. (2012). *The Situation of Public Broadcasting in Europe.* Conference: Future LRT Today: Public Broadcasting in the Changing Society. Retrieved from www.ebu.ch/CMSimages/en/Vilniusfinal0112_tcm6-73541.pdf

Lunt, P., and Livingstone, S. (2012). Media and communications regulation and the public interest. In *Media Regulation: Governance and the Interests of Citizens and Consumers* (pp. 1–17). London: Sage Publications. doi:10.4135/9781446250884.n1

McChesney, R. W., and Schiller, D. (2003). *The Political Economy of International Communications: Foundations for the Emerging Global Debate about Media Ownership and Regulation Technology, Business and Society Programme.* United Nations Research Institute for Social Development.

Nair, T. (2003). Growth and structural transformation of newspaper industry in India. *Economic and Political Weekly, 38*(39), 4182–4189.

Nair, T., and Taneja, H. (2018). Mapping and measuring media ownership and control. *Economic and Political Weekly, 53*(45), 7–8.

Narwekar, S. (1995). *Marathi Cinema in Retrospect.* Mumbai: Maharashtra Film, Stage and Cultural Development Corporation Limited.

Parker, R., and Parenta, O. (2009). Multi-level order, friction and contradiction: The evolution of Australian film industry policy. *International Journal of Cultural Policy, 15*(1), 91–105.

Parthasarathi, V. (2018). Between strategic intent and considered silence: Regulatory contours of the TV business. In *Thee Indian Media Economy: Industrial Dynamics and Cultural Adaptation* (Vol. 1, pp. 144–166).

Pendakur, M. (1985). Dynamics of cultural policy making: The U.S. film industry in India. *Journal of Communication, 35*(4), 52–72.

Ravindranath, S. (2017). GST impact on entertainment: Theatre strike in Tamil Nadu shows it is time for state government to delink itself from industry. *The Financial Express.* Retrieved from www.financialexpress.com/opinion/gst-impact-on-enter tainment-theatre-strike-in-tamil-nadu-shows-it-is-time-for-state-government-to-delink-itself-from-industry/751331/

Ross, M. R. (2010). Audiovisual laws and legal intervention in South American cinematic culture. *International Journal of Cultural Policy, 16*(4), 418–432.

Shri Ashtavinayak Cine Vision Limited v. PVR Picture Limited and Others (Case 71/2011). (2013). Competition Commission of India. Retrieved from www.cci.gov.in/sites/default/files/712011_0.pdf

Singleton, L. A., and Rockwell, S. C. (2003). Silent voices: Analyzing the FCC "media voices" criteria limiting local radio-television cross-ownership. *Communication Law and Policy, 8*(4), 385–403.

TRAI. (2014). *Recommendations on Issues Relating to Media Ownership.* New Delhi: Telecom Regulatory Authority of India.

Waterman, D. (1988). World television trade: The economic effects of privatization and new technology. *Telecommunications Policy, 12*(2), 141–151.

Wildman, S. S., and Siwek, S. E. (1988). *International Trade in Films and Television Programs.* Cambridge, MA: Ballinger Publishing Company.

5

ECONOMICS AND MANAGEMENT OF NEWSPAPER PUBLISHING

Newspaper publishing is the oldest among media industries. News publishing started after the invention of the printing press in the 16th century, and the industrialisation of Europe and America in the 19th century spurred its growth. With the spread of industrialisation and the emergence of the working classes, newspaper readership expanded to include both elites and non-elites. Around the mid-19th century, most UK and US newspapers moved from the high-priced subscription model aimed at the elites to the penny press-based mass circulation model supported by advertising. These developments led to great changes in editorial and advertising content. By the dawn of the 20th century, the ratio of editorial matter to advertising changed from about 70:30 to 50:50 (Bettig and Hall 2012, 77). The news publishing model dependent on significant revenues from advertising evolved between 1890s and 1920s in the United States. It was soon adopted in other places and continues to this day.

Currently, all over the world, newspaper businesses are facing sweeping changes in their operating environment. In a digital world, old business models are under strain and new models are still emerging, creating great uncertainty for news publishing firms. Newspaper markets in the west have been affected adversely in the last decade due to changing media consumption habits. These changed habits have resulted in the migration of advertisers to newer markets, affecting the viability of time-tested news-publishing models. However, this is not the first time that news publishing has had to cope with changes. It has faced the coming of films, radio and television and has survived all these "new" media. This chapter examines some of these issues in the Indian context and documents the changes in society and technology and their impact on the news media consumption habits of individuals, the business strategies of firms and the shape of markets. Interestingly, in a seeming contradiction, despite its waning fortunes internationally, the newspaper industry in India reveals a unique trajectory of

DOI: 10.4324/9781003199212-5

continued growth all through the second decade of the 21st century (India's Digital Future: Mass of Niches 2019, 68). Even though the newspaper business faces serious concerns about the future internationally, it is growing in India currently.

Characteristics of newspaper publishing

Newspaper publishing is characterised by high first copy costs like all other media industries. In the publishing business, the cost associated with the creation of information, which is the aspect of information production that is a public good, is called the "first copy cost." That is, to produce a new information product requires some work that is independent of how extensively the product is used. In the newspaper business, the first copy cost includes the work of reporters, writers, editors and print shop personnel that takes place before actual printing (Noll 1993, 55). Editorial, infrastructure, marketing and other overhead costs together constitute the first copy cost. Editorial costs at about 30% of the total cost are a significant part of the fixed costs of established publishers. Editorial and newsgathering departments are considered to be core competencies in India, and no established firm can afford to outsource or cut editorial costs arbitrarily. In the last few decades, advertising and circulation have also joined the list of core competencies increasing the human resource costs of news publishers.

The marginal costs in newspaper publishing are higher than in other subsectors of media because of the physical nature of the product. Even though digital versions of newspapers are becoming available, the Indian market is still dominated by the physical product. Printing costs (which include the cost of newsprint) and distribution costs constitute the marginal costs. Newsprint and printing costs of dailies are the highest, contributing to around 40% of the total cost, followed by employees at around 28% (Sindhwani 1979, 29). Marginal costs in newspaper publishing are prone to wide fluctuations due to the unpredictability in the price of newsprint. Freight costs contribute to 15% of newsprint cost which in turn depends on crude oil prices. The decline of crude oil prices also contributed to the fall in newsprint prices in the last few years. Since a significant portion of newsprint is imported, any fluctuations in the exchange rate also affect the price of newsprint. Some big newspaper groups have started hedging operations in proportion to their foreign currency exposure to reduce the risk of increase in newsprint prices (Annual Report 2015b). The central government imposed a 10% customs duty on import of newsprint in the FY 2020 Budget which will affect the print companies, and there is a possibility of increasing cover prices to cover these losses (India's Digital Future: Mass of Niches, 2019, 74).

The high first copy cost means that a new entrant to news publishing has to invest significantly. A publisher cannot vary costs according to revenues. So news publishers attempt to reduce expenditure on editorial and news gathering operations because of falling revenues. The presence of labour with low productivity gains in the content creation stage (in this case editorial staff), is seen as a prime cause of increased costs. Human resource costs of newspapers increase with the launch of new products, supplements and editions. Expansion also triggers competition as firms enter competitors' markets. This can lead to setbacks in the financials of publishers for many years. *The Hindu* newspaper suffered financially because of its burgeoning wage bill and marketing costs after it launched a Tamil-language edition and a Mumbai edition (Malik 2016) in addition to its existing English-language editions in various cities. Low productivity gains in the content creation stage can be made up by news publishers in the distribution stage, where productivity gains are progressive. But the news publishing firm should be able to increase its reach and have enough finances to survive till the productivity gains are recovered from the distribution stage. Human resource costs also go up when government-appointed wage boards recommend pay increases. The Majithia Wage Board recommendations were implemented in 2014 with great unwillingness by newspaper managements since news publishers feel that wage boards for the print industry are undesirable because no other industries have wage boards (Shooting for the Stars: Indian Media and Entertainment Industry Report 2015). Most news publishers also circumvent the implementation of wage boards by taking employees on contract.

Since fixed costs are high relative to marginal costs, news publishing enjoys economies of scale. As the circulation of a newspaper increases, its fixed costs are distributed over more copies, reducing the average cost per unit. Circulation growth increases revenues significantly. The scale benefits associated with increased production has some limitations in the case of the newspaper business because of its physical nature. Conversely, if the breakeven point is not reached by the firm for a long time, the firm will continue to make losses but will not be able to reduce costs. Newsprint costs form a significant part of marginal costs for news publishers. This has been discussed earlier as diseconomies to scale in Chapter 2. The diseconomies arrive sooner for news publishing compared to other media industries because of high marginal costs in publishing compared to broadcasting and digital media.

Overview of newspaper publishing in India

Newspaper publishing in India is highly fragmented, with multiple national and regional firms playing significant roles. Local newspapers are few and insignificant. Even though the total number of registered publications was 1,18,239 according to the Registrar of Newspapers of India (RNI) as of 31 March 2018, only 31,717 have filed their annual e-statements, suggesting that only a fourth of the registered publications are actively engaged in the business. As per the records filed with RNI, 8,930 daily newspapers were published in 2018. Among these, Hindi lead with 3,838, followed by Urdu with 1,145, Telugu with 950 and English with 815 (Press in India Report 2017–2018, 11). According to the RNI's records, the total periodicals in 2017–2018 were 21,187. Within this were 10,834 weeklies, 6,138 monthlies and 2,836 fortnightlies (Press in India Report

2017–2018, 12). Table 5.1 provides the total number of periodicals and their combined circulations.

Within the print media in India, daily newspapers form the largest segment followed by magazines of various periodicities. In revenue terms, 96% of revenues in print are made by daily newspapers in India, while all those in the magazine segment put together make just around 4% of revenues (The era of consumer A.R.T. 2020, 74). In the last few years, the circulation of general-interest magazines has taken a dip, while the circulation of niche magazines has registered positive growth. If the ownership pattern of periodical publications is examined, it reveals that most publications are owned by individuals followed by joint stock companies. Even in terms of circulation, periodicals owned by joint stock companies and individuals are far ahead of other modes of ownership (see Table 5.1). The trust model is not so popular in India. *The Tribune* from Chandigarh is the only well-known newspaper owned by a trust.

In terms of circulation figures (Table 5.2), Hindi-language dailies are ahead of all other languages. Five out of the top ten publications among dailies are

TABLE 5.1 Ownership and Circulation of Publications

Form of Ownership	No. of Newspapers	Percentage of Total	Circulation	Percentage of Circulation
Individuals	26,750	88.82	29,26,97,870	68.06
Joint Stock Companies	2,084	6.92	11,29,54,927	26.26
Firms/Partnership	215	0.71	80,56,298	1.87
Society/Association	539	1.79	73,49,058	1.71
Trusts	352	1.17	71,93,653	1.67
Government	57	0.19	8,29,498	0.19
Others	120	0.40	9,85,325	0.23
Total	30,117	100	45,05,86,219	100

Source: Press in India Report (2017–2018), RNI, pp. 70 and 73

TABLE 5.2 Top Dailies in India by Circulation

Publication	Language	Readership 2019 (000s)
Dainik Jagran	Hindi	**16,872**
Dainik Bhaskar	Hindi	**15,566**
Hindustan	Hindi	**13,213**
Amar Ujala	Hindi	**9,657**
Malayala Manorama	Malayalam	**8,569**
Daily Thanthi	Tamil	**7,379**
Lokmat	Marathi	**6,285**
Rajasthan Patrika	Hindi	**5,863**
Times of India	English	**5,560**
Mathrubhumi	Malayalam	**4,849**

Source: IRS 2019 Q4

published in Hindi. *The Times of India* (TOI) is the only English daily that figures in this list at ninth position. The Hindi-language press and the press in other Indian languages are still growing, while the English-language press is seeing declining readership in physical format due to adaption of digital platforms (Indian Readership Survey 2019, Q4).

Segmentation and profitability in the newspaper industry

Hindi and vernacular languages have been important revenue drivers in the last few years. With literacy and consumption in tier II and tier III cities and towns increasing, print media firms are spending more on Hindi and regional markets to reach out to their customers. This phase of growth is driven by 40+ cities that are experiencing economic growth, rapid urbanisation and consumption (FICCI-KPMG 2015). Major media firms like Dainik Jagran have branded themselves "unmetro" to stress the advertising yield they can offer in the growing markets. Local advertising has been a major contributor of revenues in print, as national advertising CPT (cost per thousand) is very high and also has to compete with national television (Annual Report 2015c). Table 5.3 provides details of advertising and circulation revenues in 2019 across English, Hindi and vernacular print markets.

Despite several challenges including demonetisation, shift to GST regime, implementation of RERA and an overall economic downturn, the print industry posted a growth rate of 5% in advertising revenues and 3.5% in circulation revenues.

Given the dual product nature of the business, newspaper publishers can get their revenues from either readers, advertisers or both. In most cases, newspaper publishers derive revenues both from cover price sales and advertising. Circulation revenues depend on net sale price and the number of copies sold. Advertising

TABLE 5.3 Revenues in Print Markets by Language and Segments

INR Crores	2019	Growth in 2019
English Market		
Advertising	7,380	1.5%
Circulation	3,390	−1.3%
Hindi Market		
Advertising	7,160	7.5%
Circulation	4,150	6.1%
Other language Markets		
Advertising	7,580	6.4%
Circulation	3,660	5.3%

Source: Collated from India's Digital Future: Mass of Niches, India's Media and Entertainment Report, KPMG (2019, p. 69).

TABLE 5.4 Advertising Revenues of Major Listed News Publishing Companies

Media Firms	Total Revenues (Rs Million) FY 2019–2020	Advertising Revenues (Rs Million) FY 2019–2020	Percentage of Advertising Revenues to Total Revenues
DB Corp	22,263	15,640	70.25
Jagran Prakashan	20,970	15,210	72.53
HT Media Group	21,938	17,686	80.61

Source: Company annual reports, 2019 a,b,c.

revenue depends on the net rate at which printing space is sold and the area of advertising space that is sold (Sindhwani 1979, 33). KPMG estimated total print revenues in 2019 to be around 33,300 crores out of which advertising revenues were 22,100 crores (66%) and circulation revenues were 11,200 crores (34%). The rise in circulation revenues is attributed to increasing expansion of regional-language editions in small towns and hinterlands. With the Compounded Annual Growth Rate (CAGR) prediction of 4.2% in total revenues for the period 2019–2024, the KPMG report suggests the possibility of organic growth in the near future. This is a positive scenario when compared to other countries where news publishers are facing declining and negative growth rates.

A cursory look at the revenues of some leading listed news publishers (Table 5.4) is sufficient to demonstrate that advertising drives the revenues of news publishers. In 2019–2020, DB Corp, which publishes *Dainik Bhaskar*, earned 70.25% of its revenues from advertising, while the Jagran Prakashan group, which publishes *Dainik Jagran*, earned 72.53% and the Hindustan Group that publishes *Hindustan Times* earned 80.61% from advertising.

For strategic purposes, news publishers do not ignore circulation revenues while pursuing advertising revenues. The two sources of revenue are not independent of each other but interdependent. For instance, in its annual report, DB Corp mentions that increasing circulation revenues was one of its strategic initiatives. This "was driven with an objective to demonstrate to advertisers the rationale behind our insistence on better advertising yields, where consumer price was an effective and irrefutable barometer" (Annual Report 2015a, 14). News publishers want to demonstrate to advertisers that their readers have greater per capita purchasing power.

Strategic management of newspaper firms

News publishers have to take many strategic decisions in the short and long term to survive competition and be profitable. The technologies they invest in, the revenue and pricing policies they adopt and the way they engage with the competition would significantly affect their finances. We can broadly classify them as strategies to increase market share, strategies to maximise revenues and strategies to cut costs. Even though the number of newspapers seems to be very high, a close look will reveal that the competition is oligopolistic, with different degrees of concentration. Language and geography play an important role in newspaper markets (Nair 2003). For instance, among English-language dailies, only three publications cross the 10 lakhs mark in circulation. In Hindi, one publication is above the 40-lakh mark in circulation, one above the 30-lakh mark and two that cross the 20-lakh mark. Among non-Hindi languages, nine publications across the country cross the 10-lakhs mark in readership (Highest Circulated Dailies, Weeklies & Magazines amongst Member Publications (across Languages) 2019). Given the importance of audience markets for advertisers, most of the strategies of news publishers to increase market share would be through increasing circulation and readership. A range of strategies are adapted by Indian news publishers to increase market share.

Strategies to increase market share

Market share can be increased through either organic or inorganic growth. News publishers can choose to increase the circulation of the current product or launch a new product in the case of organic growth. In the case of inorganic growth, news publishers acquire other publishers to increase their market share. TOI has increased its editions across the country to increase its market share organically in the last decade. It has also launched new products like *Mumbai Mirror* and *Bangalore Mirror* and acquired *Vijaya Times* in Bangalore to increase its market share inorganically.

Market share for existing titles can be increased through price competition or non-price competition. Generally, competing newspapers are priced in the same range. When a competitor reduces its cover price to increase circulation, competing papers will be forced to reduce cover prices, leading to a collective loss of circulation revenues for the industry. Reduction of prices also affects newspaper agents and newspaper vendors as they are paid a percentage of the cover price as commission. In such situations, the rate of commission has to be reworked to compensate for their loss; otherwise, delivery channel partners will be unhappy. Price competition does not happen often, as it leads to collective loss and disruptions in the market structure.

The English news publishing market in India in the 1990s offers a good example for subscription price competition. Till the 1990s, English-language newspaper markets in India were similar to their US counterparts. Each geographical market was led by one newspaper. The *Hindustan Times* (HT) in Delhi, the *Times of India* (TOI) in Mumbai, *The Hindu* in Chennai, *The Telegraph* in Calcutta, *The Tribune* in Chandigarh, the *Deccan Chronicle* in Hyderabad and the *Deccan Herald* in Bangalore used to be the leaders in their respective markets. They were near monopolies in each of their geographical markets. This cosy equilibrium was disrupted by the TOI when it launched its editions in Delhi and Bangalore. This led to a multi-cornered competition to gain a significant share of readers in the national markets. The New Delhi leader, HT launched its Mumbai edition. The Hyderabad leader, *Deccan Chronicle*, launched its Chennai edition, as Hindu was already in Hyderabad. To thwart the HT and DNA in Mumbai, TOI launched its second title, *Mumbai Mirror*, and launched a price war. In 1994, TOI reduced its cover price from INR 2.30 to INR 1.50 in the Delhi market. As TOIs circulation increased, HT took the price competition further in 1999 by slashing the price from INR 1.50 to INR 1.00; TOI followed suit. TOI started combo offers by bundling with the *Economic Times*. At the end of the price war, TOI emerged as more successful by becoming a national player with increased circulation and readership. Now the broadsheet market is back to what appears to be near collaborative pricing. During such a period, news publishers compete for advertising revenues and enjoy stable revenues. During the period of price competition, the player with deep pockets will survive and benefit later with the increased market share. From an economics point of view, one would like to know how much of a price reduction would make a loyal reader switch to a competitor. This can be attempted by measuring the price elasticity of demand and the cross-elasticity of demand of respective newspapers. Price elasticity of demand can be measured by dividing the percentage of change in circulation to percentage of change in price. Cross-elasticity of demand can be measured by dividing the percentage of change in circulation for title A with the percentage of change in price for title B. However, these measures are difficult to arrive at most times, as relevant data is not available.

Non-price competition among news publishers happens through content changes, design changes, promotional campaigns, etc. All these activities are expensive. Sometimes all these activities are done together to reposition the paper or increase market share raising the total costs significantly.

Cost reduction strategies

Cost reduction strategies have become very important for news publishers facing a decrease in their share of advertising revenues. News publishers have realised that they need not compete all the time. There are spheres of activity where all the firms in the market would be better off through cooperation rather than competition. Of late, some news publishers have been cooperating to cut costs. Within the perceived core competencies of news publishers, editorial and news-gathering activities do not suit for cooperation, whereas printing, pre-press and transport can be shared or outsourced. Cooperation in these areas does not attract the attention of regulators such as the Competition Commission. This is not similar to collusive pricing, which would attract penal measures from the regulators. There are clear economies of scale available to printers and publishers if they print competing papers at the same printing facility. Competing newspapers have been using the services of the same printer in certain geographical markets. For instance, *Lokmat* prints for its competitor *Maharashtra Times* at its Aurangabad facility (FICCI-KPMG 2015, 55). If trust issues are solved, news publishers can cut costs through cooperation in non-core areas. Even within editorial and news gathering, syndication and news agencies businesses have developed historically to reduce the respective costs. Another way is to lobby collectively with the government to reduce or remove taxes. For instance, all the news publishers have been collectively representing to the government through the Indian Newspaper Society (INS) and Indian Newsprint Manufacturers Association (INMA) to not impose VAT on newsprint. Already, newspapers do not attract sales tax in view of its being excluded from the definition of "goods" under section 2d of Central Sales Tax Act, 1956.

Cost reduction strategies at the firm level are also very important. While collective strategies help the whole industry, firm-level strategies are needed to compete with other firms. Tight budgetary planning and control have become very important. News publishers who have multiple media properties, especially in television and digital, are trying to reduce costs by setting up integrated newsrooms that provide text, images and video content seamlessly for multiple media platforms. The news operations of Zee group, India Today group and CNBC-TV 18 are making attempts to integrate their newsrooms through which they expect to reduce their operational costs and manpower costs significantly (FICCI-KPMG 2015, 55). This would involve investments in new technologies and re-skilling existing staff.

Revenue maximisation strategies

Due to increasing competition from other media, the advertising revenue share of print media has been gradually decreasing over the years. It dropped from 79% in 1984 to 70% in 1990 and to 66% in 1992 (Kothari 1995, 60). After liberalisation, due to increased competition from satellite television and later due to digital media, it fell further to 49% in 2005, to 42.5% in 2014 and to 31.89% in 2019. Even though the print revenues have been shrinking in terms of shares, it continues to grow in absolute terms year on year since the overall media pie has been growing in India. Since a significant part of news publishers revenues come from advertising, it has become necessary to focus on strategies for effective advertising management.

Advertising revenues of news publishers can be broadly classified into display advertising, classified advertising, public notices and legal advertising. Like in other countries, display advertising in India has been facing serious competition from television, while classified advertising has been facing competition from digital media. In response to television, news publishers have ramped up their quality of printing with state-of-the-art printing presses to attract display advertising. To retain their classified advertisers, news publishers have moved their print brands to digital space. Public notices and legal advertising are steadier sources as they are mandated by law. It includes information notices regarding laws, election matters, bankruptcy notices, bid lettings and so on (Kothari 1995, 63). The advertising section has to be in touch with attorneys, courts and governments to collect these advertisements. However, the Indian government, which is the biggest advertiser through its Department of Audio-Visual Publicity (DAVP), pays discounted rates when compared to market rates. DAVP is the nodal advertising agency for all the departments and ministries of the Government of India, besides public sector undertakings and autonomous bodies. The Directorates of Information and Public Relations (DIPRs) under state governments also follow DAVP rates. In August 2020, the government notified its new print media advertisement policy.

News publishers also cooperate to increase revenues in various ways. In a given newspaper market, all the competitors can discreetly agree to increase the price of their respective newspapers and peg them at the same price or in the same range. Such strategies help these firms increase their subscription revenues, which are still a smaller part of their revenues. Collaborative pricing is seen as evidence of cartelisation by government regulators if the price hike is too steep. Products like cement and steel have been prone to such situations forcing government intervention. However, news publishers have never increased their prices high enough to attract intervention. For instance, in Hyderabad, all the English broadsheets are priced between INR 6 and INR 7, and all the leading Telugu newspapers are priced at INR 5, suggesting that collaborative pricing is in practice among competing publishers. Whenever newsprint prices go up, competing publishers show more interest in cooperative pricing to recover their variable costs and shore up their bottom line.

Cooperation among news publishers in different geographic and language markets also works for bundling audiences to provide a national market. The "Oneindia initiative" by the *Hindustan Times*, *The Hindu* and the Ananda Bazar Patrika (ABP) group brings together three English dailies and three language dailies in Hindi, Bengali and Tamil to offer a common platform for selling advertising space. The group offers bundled advertisements at a discounted price in all newspapers which are part of the group. It not only offers the advertisers a near pan-Indian coverage in a single window, but it also offers the members of the group collective bargaining strength that they cannot enjoy as individual players. Such alliances also bolster the viability of print media as a competitive advertising platform in a multi-cornered competition

Challenge from digital media

Digital media has been identified as the single biggest challenge for news publishers in the last two decades. Even though news publishers have faced competition from radio and television earlier, the digital threat seems to be different. Radio and television were competing media that produced their own content to suit the needs of the medium. They also depended on print media to a large extent, enhancing its credibility. Many television and radio shows are centred on the original content produced in print media. Digital media does not merely compete but appears to be appropriating print. As a distribution medium, it rides on print content. News aggregators are a major problem in the online space, as they do not invest in original news production. Even though news publishers are getting a lot of audience on digital platforms, they are not able to make revenues because they have lost control over the value chain. With their ability to control networks, platform and hardware digital media owners take a significant share of the revenues. The overall decline in the revenues of news publishers is seen as a threat to investment in original news production.

However, it is also identified as an opportunity. Online presence is increasingly being seen as complementary to printed newspapers. News publishers foresee a future, where they may have to continue both online and offline models. Even if the circulation of the current physical product falls to 25% of the total circulation, the print version may have to be continued to make it available to the segment that prefers it in that mode. Even though online investments are not giving returns, news publishers have to keep investing and innovating as the space and business models develop. They have to ensure that all the possible stakeholders in the value chain migrate to the digital space. The greatest asset they have is the brand, and they have to ensure that the brand's transition to the digital space happens smoothly.

The Independent, in the UK, is the first daily newspaper to go completely digital with its site independent.co.uk in April 2016. The publishers claimed that this move helps them save costs and invest in high-quality editorial to attract readers online. The strategy seems to have paid off, as it made profits consecutively for three years and even overtook *The Telegraph* in 2020. News is offered as a bundled product when delivered as a physical product. When it is delivered on digital distribution platforms, it can be unbundled, offering some advantages to publishers. If the content is compelling, it will open possibilities for micropayments. Experiments globally for paywalls and micropayments in journalism have not been successful. Blendle, a tech start-up from the Netherlands, claims that it has 60,000 subscribers and hundreds of thousands of users of its micropayment option. Blendle, which positioned itself as the "iTunes of journalism," tries to bring all the top newspapers and magazines on one platform so that the readers can have a choice and pay only for what they want to read instead of being forced to pay for the bundled product. The revenues are shared 70:30 between the publisher and the platform. They also offer limited refunds to readers who are not satisfied. The platform recently announced that its micropayments strategy has not been successful and that they wish to move towards premium subscriptions. New York-based Magzter, which calls itself a cross-platform, self-service, global digital newsstand, has tied up with leading publishers from across the world and distributes thousands of magazines in multiple languages. Magzter's gold subscription option offers unlimited access to its magazines on the lines of OTT platforms. It also has a lite version wherein the subscribers can choose five magazines. Besides revenue sharing, this platform also shares customer data with the publishers. The business and revenue models are still evolving in the space and slowly providing digital revenue streams to the beleaguered publishers. In India, in the English-language market, *The Hindu* offers its e-paper on subscription at INR 1199 for one year and INR 699 for three months. *The Caravan* magazine offers its annual digital subscriptions at INR 1200.

While the digital media are seen as a threat in the west, it is only seen as a segment of the market in India at the present time, especially by Hindi and regional-language newspapers. The classified advertising revenues of Indian print players are small, and they have not yet migrated to the digital space, especially in Hindi and regional-language markets. Digital is seen by many players as another medium, to reach out to audiences who could not be reached earlier because of the limitations of the physical product. News portals, e-papers, mobile apps and social media are being increasingly used to reach out those who cannot be reached with the physical product. The new "touch points" are being actively nurtured. Diaspora and people living in other parts of the country are being reached through the digital versions by language newspapers. A younger demographic is being reached though digital platforms as they are not interested in using the physical product. In the Indian market, English newspapers are losing a section of their physical sales to digital versions compared to Hindi and vernacular papers. News publishing firms believe that both segments can develop further without cannibalising each other, at least in the near future. In that sense, digital and print are seen as complementary to each other.

In disruptive situations like the one being faced due to the arrival of new technologies, news media publishers have to innovate at various levels, at the level of the product, process and also with their business models (Where News? 2006). However, with the digital landscape continuously evolving, strategic decision making has been very difficult. As innovations continue, no long-term predictions can be made, and most of the strategic decisions have to be made for the short term. The focus on the short term means a lot of firm's resources and energy will be spent on survival and adaptability. This is still very much a time of transition, and Indian newspaper firms continue to show growth in their revenues.

References

#ShootingfortheStars: Indian Media and Entertainment Industry Report. (2015). FICCI-KPMG. Retrieved January 6, 2020, from https://assets.kpmg/content/dam/kpmg/pdf/2015/03/FICCI-KPMG_2015.pdf

Annual Report. (2015a). DB Corp. Retrieved February 17, 2020, from https://storage.googleapis.com/webimages.dbcorp.in/investor/Annual%20Report%20FY%2014-15.pdf

Annual Report. (2015b). Hindustan Media Ventures Limited (HMVL). Retrieved March 5, 2021, from www.hmvl.in/pdf/ANNUAL_REPORT_2014-15.pdf (February 17, 2020).

Annual Report. (2015c). Jagaran Prakashan. Retrieved February 17, 2020, from https://jplcorp.in/new/pdf/annualreportjplalongwithformA_1415.pdf

Annual Report. (2019a). DB Corp. Retrieved February 17, 2020, from https://storage.googleapis.com/webimages.dbcorp.in/investor/Annual%20Report%20FY%202018-19.pdf

Annual Report. (2019b). Hindustan Media Ventures Limited (HMVL). Retrieved February 17, 2020, from www.hmvl.in/pdf/Annual_Report_2018_19.pdf

Annual Report. (2019c). Jagaran Prakashan. Retrieved February 17, 2020, from https://jplcorp.in/new/pdf/Annual_Report_2018-2019.pdf

Bettig, R. V., and Hall, J. L. (2012). *Big Media, Big Money: Cultural Texts and Political Economics.* Lanham: Rowman and Littlefield Publishers.

The era of consumer A.R.T. (2020). India's Media and Entertainment Sector, Ficci – E&Y Report. Retrieved June 7, 2021, from https://ficci.in/spdocument/23200/FICCI-EY-Report-media-and-entertainment-2020.pdf

Highest Circulated Dailies, Weeklies & Magazines amongst Member Publications (across Languages). (2019). Audit Bureau of Circulations. Retrieved March 25, 2020, from www.auditbureau.org/files/JD%202019%20Highest%20Circulated%20(across%20languages).pdf

Indian Readership Survey 2019 Q4. (2019). Media Research Users Council India. Retrieved May 4, 2020 from https://mruc.net/uploads/posts/ab71f971df5abf07040e1435bf4fcfe3.pdf

India's Digital Future: Mass of Niches (India's Media and Entertainment Report). (2019). KPMG. Retrieved May 4, 2020, from https://assets.kpmg/content/dam/kpmg/in/pdf/2019/08/india-media-entertainment-report-2019.pdf

Kothari, G. (1995). *Newspaper Management in India.* Netherlands: Intercultural Open University, Jaipur: Rajasthan Patrika.

Malik, A. (2016). The Hindu's troubled financials. *The Hoot.* Retrieved May 6, 2020, from http://asu.thehoot.org/media-watch/media-business/the-hindus-troubled-financials-9174

Nair, T. (2003). Growth and structural transformation of newspaper industry in India. *Economic and Political Weekly, 38*(39), 4182–4189.

Noll, R. G. (1993). The economics of information: A user's guide. *The Knowledge Economy: The Nature of Information in the 21st Century.* Queenstown, MD: Aspen Institute.

Press in India Report. (2017–2018). Office of Registrar of Newspapers for India. Retrieved June 10, 2020, from http://rni.nic.in/all_page/pin201718.htm

Sindhwani, T. N. (1979). *Newspaper Economics and Management.* New Delhi: Ankur Publishing House.

Where News? Report 1: Business Models of Newspaper Publishing Companies. (2006). World Association of News Publishers. Retrieved from http://m.wan-ifra.org/reports/2006/05/01/where-news-report-1-business-models-of-newspaper-publishing-companies

6

ECONOMICS AND MANAGEMENT OF TELEVISION BROADCASTING

Broadcasting is a mechanism to distribute content (also referred to as programming or software), to audiences. The content can be audio only, as in the case of radio, or it can be audiovisual, as in the case of television. We focus on the economics and management of television broadcasting in this chapter. Although the term broadcast television is generally used to refer to free-to-air terrestrial transmission of the signal in some countries, it is used in India to include delivery of audiovisual content via cable and satellite as well.

We begin this chapter by examining the economic characteristics of television broadcasting in the first section and then move onto a brief overview of television broadcasting in India in the second section. The third section focuses on the market segments in television broadcasting, and the fourth section deals with revenue streams and pricing strategies. The fifth section details product lifecycle management in broadcasting with regard to format, quality, price, syndication and dubbing. The sixth section presents key challenges facing this industry, such as increasing content costs, dependence on advertising revenues, distribution bottlenecks, carriage fees, digitisation, average revenues per user (ARPU) and consolidation. The seventh section discusses distribution and marketing strategies such as regionalisation, bouquetisation and bundling, and the final section explores scheduling strategies in multi-channel environments and the limits and problems of competitive scheduling strategies.

Economic characteristics of television broadcasting

The economic problem of excludability is a key factor in the history of the television industry and has shaped the industry in fundamental ways (Delong and Froomkin 2000). Free-to-air terrestrial television broadcasting offers a prime example of the free-rider problem in economics, i.e., how to exclude someone

DOI: 10.4324/9781003199212-6

who has not paid for the programming. Theatrical distribution of films offers the opportunity to earn revenues through the ticket purchased by the individual at the theatre box office, but no such opportunities exist for television producers or distributors since the terrestrial television broadcast signal that is received at the viewer's home is a public good which is non-rivalrous (i.e., consumption by one user does not prevent its consumption by another user) and non-excludable (it is not possible to prevent users from accessing it). As Noll (1993) points out, "If one person decides to view a television program, the other viewers of the program experience neither an additional cost nor diminished access to the program" (p. 30).

As we know, public goods have a high first copy cost compared to their dissemination costs. This is particularly true of television broadcasting, where the entire expenditure of programme creation and transmission needs to be borne before the first consumer is reached. Some countries (including India, for a brief while) did manage to impose the requirement of a licence for each television receiver, but if revenues cannot be collected from viewers, then how can television production be economically sustainable?

Historically, there have been two solutions to raise the funding required for television production and distribution. The first is through government participation, i.e., state ownership of television transmission and production infrastructure. Government presence in television production and distribution has been popular in Europe and some parts of Asia, including India, China and Japan, and it places the focus on programmes that governments, rather than audiences, are eager to view. The second solution has been advertising. The reliance on advertising has been blamed for commodification of the audience (Smythe 1977) and the descent into "lowest-common-denominator" programming—since advertisers are interested in reaching the largest possible audiences and television channels end up creating programming that would bring in advertising revenue—rather than programming that would be meaningful to their viewers (Delong and Froomkin 2000). Both these solutions are sub-optimal, as they bring with them their own set of market distortions.

The problem of excludability gives us a clue to understanding the spread of cable and satellite distribution. The cable and the direct-to-home (DTH) satellite dish offer the means to exclude free riders. Access is restricted to paid users, allowing television broadcasting firms to earn revenues through subscription fees (Noll 1993).

Overview of television broadcasting in India

Television broadcasting in India started well after many other countries and reached large national audiences only in the 1980s. The history of television in India for the first three decades is the history of the government broadcaster. While experimental transmissions had begun in 1959, and daily transmissions in 1965, television was restricted to New Delhi in this decade. It was only in 1972 that a second station was commissioned in Mumbai. The decade of the 1970s is best known for the Satellite Instructional Television Experiment, when a NASA satellite was used to broadcast development programmes to rural audiences from August 1975 to 31 July 1976. In 1976 the government television broadcaster Doordarshan was created as a unit separate from the radio broadcaster All India Radio of which it was a part. In 1982 colour television was introduced with the New Delhi Asian Games. As Athique (2009) points out, the irony of television content in these years was that much of it was aimed at rural audiences when penetration was mainly in urban, middle-class households.

Private enterprise in the television sector started when cable television was introduced by local entrepreneurs who strung up unauthorised cables and collected payments in cash from the late 1980s onwards. The coming of liberalisation in the 1990s energised television broadcasting in India. In what was popularly referred to as the "invasion from the sky," Indian and international satellite broadcasters uplinked programming that was received at cable head ends using large dish antennae and delivered through the last mile of cable to consumers. Government restrictions on direct-to-home satellite services were lifted in the next decade, and the Indian television market now includes free-to-air terrestrial broadcasting by the government-owned broadcaster, DTH, satellite broadcasts delivered via cable and Internet-based television programming which can be accessed on smartphones.

According to the government's Economic Survey (2015–2016) released as a part of the Union Budget in 2016, India has 168 million television households and overtook the United States in 2015 to become the world's second largest television market after China. Television programming in India today, at the beginning of the third decade of the 21st century includes entertainment, news and films, and they are supported through both advertising and subscription revenues. A variety of both imported and domestically produced genres are present. We examine these market segments in detail in the next section.

The additional complexity in the Indian television industry that sets it apart from television industries around the world is that it is available in a large number of languages. Language markets range from the nationally available English and Hindi-language channels to the smaller regional-language channels. Mumbai, Chennai, Calcutta and Hyderabad are some of the centres of television production. Unionised crews operate in all these centres to create programming for the 24-hour television channels.

Political parties and individual politicians own stakes in various segments of the television industry, including cable distribution, that gives them the power to decide what information reaches the audience and deserves critical attention in a democracy (Parthasarathi and Srinivas 2016). Ownership of television production and distribution channels is an important area of research from a public policy and political economy perspective, especially in India where the large majority of the population depends on audiovisual media for its news.

Unlike the film industry, where every film has to receive a certificate from the Central Board of Film Certification before it can be exhibited, the television industry is self-regulating when it comes to content through two industry bodies, the News Broadcasting Standards Authority and the Indian Broadcasting Foundation, which focus on content-related complaints pertaining to news and entertainment respectively. The sectoral regulator for the television broadcasting industry is the Telecom Regulatory Authority of India (TRAI) along with its Telecom Disputes Settlement and Appellate Tribunal (TDSAT).

Television broadcasting—market segments

Content production, broadcasting and distribution are the three segments of the television industry as acknowledged by the Ministry of Information and Broadcasting (Annual Report 2015). Both the government and privately owned corporations participate in all three segments of the industry. Such is the pace of growth in this dynamic industry that anything that is written about television in India runs the risk of being outdated by the time it reaches the reader. Given this frenetic pace of change, this chapter aims to capture a snapshot of these three segments of the industry in the middle of the decade of the 2010s.

Content production takes place through private content producers who are unregulated. This content is then aggregated by broadcasters who broadcast this content on the channels in their network. In 2014, India's broadcasting segment had approximately 847 television channels that packaged and uplinked content (Annual Report 2016), by the end of 2019, this had grown to 918 channels (Annual Report 2020). Based on their business models, television channels are divided into two groups—free-to-air channels that constitute about 75% of all channels and focus solely on advertising to earn their revenues, and pay channels (approximately 25% of all channels) that earn subscription revenues in addition to advertising revenues (Annual Report 2015). Thus, advertising is the major revenue for this segment of the industry, as we can see from the estimated revenues. In 2019, the broadcasting segment of the television industry was estimated to have earned INR 37,200 crores, of which approximately 67% was from advertising revenues and the remaining 33% came from subscription. From a genre point of view, general entertainment channels in Hindi and other languages contributed the highest share of viewers, 58% in 2015; while Hindi and regional-language films followed with 20% viewership on television (The Future 2016).

Four types of distribution services have been approved by the government in India—cable, direct-to-home (DTH), Internet Protocol Television (IPTV) and Headend in the Sky (HITS). In 2014, the distribution segment consisted of 6,000 multi-system operators (MSOs) who downlinked and decrypted signals, 60,000 local cable operators (LCOs) who provided last mile connectivity and 7 DTH/satellite TV providers (Annual Report 2016).

The government offers a DTH service through Doordarshan. In addition, six private corporations offer DTH services—Dish TV, Tata Sky, Sun Direct TV, Reliance Big TV, Airtel Digital TV and Videocon d2h. The prices of these services are regulated by the government through TRAI.

The Government of India also has a strong presence in the television industry through Doordarshan, which is a vertically integrated content producer, broadcaster and distributor. As a broadcaster, it aggregates content which it sometimes also commissions from private television producers. Doordarshan distributes its channels via terrestrial, satellite and DTH transmission networks which it owns. In 2015, Doordarshan's offerings included 5 all-India channels, 16 regional channels, 11 state networks and one international channel, i.e., a total of 33 satellite channels that reached 92% of India's population through 1416 transmitters (Annual Report 2015). As a government broadcaster, Doordarshan channels are free-to-air and must be carried by all other distributors in the country. State governments also offer cable television distribution services like the Arasu cable network in Tamil Nadu.

The government's policy of implementing Digitally Accessible Systems (DAS) has resulted in the generation of enormous entertainment tax revenues for the government, and broadcasters also gained from the dual benefit of lower carriage fees to MSOs and higher subscription revenues (Annual Report 2016). Digital systems allow for many more channels to be carried, thereby reducing MSOs' ability to demand carriage fees from broadcasters. Digital systems also bring transparency to declaration of subscribers there by allowing broadcasters to mop up higher subscription revenues.

Foreign Direct Investment (FDI) of 26% is allowed in television content production, and 74% is allowed in television distribution (Economic Survey 2015).

Revenue streams and pricing strategies in television broadcasting

The main revenue streams for Indian television are advertising and subscriptions. Of these two streams, due to the penetration of pay television channels, the major share of revenues come from subscriptions. In 2015, the television industry in India is estimated to have earned an approximate total of INR 54,200 crores. Of this approximately 67% (INR 36,100 crores) is attributed to subscription revenues and 33% (INR 18,100 crores) to advertising revenues (The Future 2016). Within four years these estimates had grown to total revenues of approximately INR 71,400 crores of which 65% (INR 46,300) came from subscription and 35% (INR 25,100) came from advertising (A Year 2020). Cricket advertising is a valuable contributor to television revenues from advertising with the ICC World Cup contributing an estimated INR 600 crores and the IPL contributing approximately INR 850 crores in 2015 (The Future 2016). In 2018, IPL is estimated to have contributed approximately INR 1,800 crores to television advertising revenues (A Year 2020). Television broadcasters are beginning geo-targeting of audiences so that advertisers can reach India's culturally diverse television audiences, i.e., deliver advertising based on the location of audiences so that smaller regional advertisers are also able to use television (The Future 2016).

Other sources of revenues include SMS/voice voting and show integrations. To increase viewer engagement, SMS voting was primarily adopted by game shows and news programmes where viewers could vote by sending text messages to a predetermined number to choose a particular contestant or point of view. Viewers who sent text messages for SMS voting paid premium rates, with each SMS costing from INR 2 to INR 5 (TRAI puts ceiling 2012). Broadcasters received up to 25% of the revenue earned per SMS (Bansal 2004). Most non-fiction programming, including game shows and talent shows such as *Kaun Banega Crorepati, Indian Idol, India's Got Talent, Nach Baliye* and many others, provided an SMS voting option. *Indian Idol*, in its third edition in 2007, earned crores of rupees through SMS and voice votes (Parbat and Nag 2007). *Kaun Banega Crorepati* had earned SMS revenues even before the show went on air because participants were recruited through their SMS response to a question that was broadcast (Vasi 2005). The *Har Seat Hot Seat* lucky draw of Kaun *Banega Crorepati*, where audiences responded to a question via SMS to get a shot at a INR 2 lakh prize generated such enormous revenues that it was judged to be an unfair trade practice by the National Consumer Commission and resulted in fines for the broadcaster Star Plus and telecom partner Airtel (Star Plus Airtel 2008). In 2012, the regulator TRAI imposed a ceiling on the premium rates that telecom companies could charge for SMS voting (TRAI puts ceiling 2012)

Like product placements in films, "show integrations" generate revenues through the promotion of films on television shows. Typically, show integrations feature performances by the cast of the film that is being promoted within the format of the television show. For instance, the cast of Hindi films *Sarabjit* and *Housefull 3* were featured in performances on the popular Hindi television comedy *The Kapil Sharma Show* to promote these films before their release in May 2016.

Broadcasters are also able to earn some additional revenues through the syndication of television content in national and international markets in the same language or through language dubbed versions for some years after its first telecast. The following section discusses these streams in detail.

Product lifecycle management in broadcasting—*format, quality, price syndication and dubbing*

Since media products are non-rivalrous in their consumption, once a television show has been broadcast, it does not lose all value. Depending on the type of television programme, a variety of "aftermarkets" provide additional revenue streams to the content rights holder. Chris (2006) defines repurposing as "multiple exposures through same-day, same-week or same-month encores, usually on cable channels" (p. 66). Indian television viewers will be familiar with this practice which is followed by a number of cable and satellite channels that repeat their programmes within a 24-hour and weekly schedule generally at off-prime times in the afternoon or in the middle of the night.

Repurposing or repeats can take place across channels as well. As Keane and Moran (2008) observe, "Cross-platform delivery has become a means of survival for commercial broadcasters. In contemporary media industries it makes economic sense to repurpose content across platforms, increasing opportunities to accrue intellectual property rents" (p. 165). This has been tried in India. For instance, in 2004, the broadcaster Star India, in a horizontal integration move, launched Star Utsav, a free-to-air channel targeted at audiences in smaller towns that would feature reruns of its flagship Star Plus channel's Hindi-language shows (Star India's FTA 2004). This would allow Star India to take its shows (that were launched when cable and satellite television penetration in India was much lower) to the new audiences who were being added each year as cable and satellite penetration increased. On Doordarshan, popular shows such as *Ramayan* and *Mahabharat* were rerun (many decades after their first run) when shooting for television shows was halted due to the COVID-19 pandemic in the year 2020.

Broadcasters also syndicate television shows to international markets. In 2000, Star Plus launched Star Plus UK, its channel in the United Kingdom that broadcast shows that had previously aired on its Indian channel. Rights to individual television shows are also sold to broadcasters in other countries. Revenues are also generated from language-dubbed versions of successful Hindi serials that are broadcast in other Indian languages. Generally, this is of shows that are produced in the largest market, the Hindi-language market, and language dubbed into regional languages. A number of shows from the Hindi Star Plus channel are dubbed into Tamil and shown on the Tamil channel Star Vijay.

Another revenue stream comes from the franchising of successful television show formats which now have an international market. Keane and Moran (2008) identify the advantages of format franchises as follows:

> A program can be reformatted in different territories and the local producer or broadcaster can access a template that has already withstood two rounds of R&D—first, to survive development and trialing before broadcasting executives; and secondly, further testing before viewing audiences. Recycling successful TV program ideas takes much of the guesswork out of local television production in many lower cost genres. In this sense, it is a low risk strategy in an industry, which as we have noted above, that is averse to risk-taking.
>
> *(p. 157)*

A number of popular television shows in India, such as *Kaun Banega Crorepati*, *Indian Idol* and *India's Got Talent*, are franchises of international formats.

Home video is not a popular revenue stream for Indian television shows. Although some television shows such as the popular mythological series *Ramayan* and *Mahabharat*; and sitcoms such as *Sarabhai vs Sarabhai* and *Yeh Jo Hai Zindagi* have made the transition to home video, they are the exceptions rather than the norm.

Key challenges—*increasing content costs, dependence on advertising revenues, distribution bottlenecks, carriage fees, digitisation of broadcast industry, higher ARPU, consolidation in the broadcast industry*

Content costs in the television industry have been increasing, in part because of the proliferation of television channels and the reliance on a handful of content production companies (Kohli-Khandekar 2011). While the increase in the numbers of television channels shows us that there is a great demand for television content, we also need to note that television content production is intellectual property creation that requires specialised inputs and also carries a strong element of risk. To reduce risk, buyers tend to prefer established production houses that have proved themselves in the past. This allows established production houses to negotiate better prices for their products, thus resulting in increased content costs.

As we have seen earlier, a television broadcasters' revenues comes from advertising as well as subscription. Thus, television broadcasters would like as wide a reach as possible for their programmes since reach determines advertising rates. Analog distribution systems suffer from a constraint on signal-carrying capacity. While established channels may not have a problem reaching audiences, this scarcity acts as a barrier to entry which gives MSOs the upper hand while negotiating higher carriage fees from new channels which have to convince MSOs to carry their signal.

From 2012 onwards the government mandated the roll-out of an ambitious digital access system (DAS) in India in a phased manner spreading from metro areas to smaller towns and rural areas. The main benefit of digital distribution is that it overcomes the capacity constraint that analogue systems suffer from, thereby easing distribution bottlenecks. Carriage fees are thus expected to decline with digitisation, as MSOs will be able to carry a larger number of channels (Carriage Fee 2014).

Average revenues per user (ARPU) measures the total revenues earned by the MSOs and DTH companies divided by the number of their users. Analog distribution made it relatively easy for opacity to be maintained about the actual number of users, and some estimates put the disclosure rate as low as 20% (Agnihotri 2002), creating a challenge for MSOs and broadcasters to realise subscription revenues. Digitisation of distribution increases transparency at the last mile and can translate into increased ARPU for broadcasters and MSOs as well as generate higher tax revenues for the government. Digitisation also allows for sharper market segmentation (Khanna, cited in Agnihotri 2002), allowing MSOs to offer personalised packages to high-value consumers and increase their ARPU. By 2013, broadcasters and MSOs were already seeing higher ARPUs as a result of the completion of the first two phases of the DAS in India (Tiwari 2013). In 2016, urban cable MSOs and DTH distributors claimed an ARPU of INR 250 (Digitise India 2016).

While India has a large number of television channels, they belong to a small number of broadcasters since the industry is highly consolidated. In 2012, five broadcasters—Star India, Sony, Network 18, the Sun group and the Zee group—dominated the television broadcasting industry, accounting for almost 65% of audience viewership (Kohli-Khandekar 2012). In 2014, Reliance Industries consolidated its stakes in Network 18 and Eenadu Television's Hindi news channels that catered to Uttar Pradesh, Madhya Pradesh, Bihar and Rajasthan as well as stakes in other ETV channels (Network 18 2014).

Distribution and marketing strategies—regionalisation as a strategy, bouquetisation, bundling

Regional markets play an important role in television broadcasting in India to the extent that "key players in the media industries (are) now imagining the media markets in India almost entirely through a regional framework" (Kumar 2014, 27). In 2015, while Hindi-language channels had the highest viewership in the country, Tamil- (25.7%) and Telugu- (24.4%) language channels dominated the regional-language markets in terms of viewership (The Future 2016). TV viewership shares in languages other than Hindi, Tamil, Telugu, Kannada and Malayalam increased from 15% in 2016 to 23% in 2019 and viewership of Bhojpuri, Urdu and Gujarati went up by 200%, 179% and 157% respectively (A Year 2020). The entry of private broadcasters is considered to be foundational to the growth in regional-language television broadcasting (Parthasarathi and Srinivas 2012).

> Just as sound pictures had led to multiple production centers and distinct vernacular markets in cinema in the 1930s and 1940s, the freeing of television from the Hindi-centric policies of Doordarshan paved the way for the emergence of large regional players in Indian television.
>
> *(Athique 2009, 163)*

Advertisers wanting to reach audiences in smaller towns where media consumption is growing alongside market saturation and slowing consumption in metropolitan areas are seen as the twin forces that are driving the acquisition of regional media companies by the large national broadcasters (Kumar 2014). "Regional presence enables national networks to offer a wider bouquet to advertisers and thereby, provides them with higher bargaining power" (Shashidhar 2015).

Especially when it comes to news, regional-language news channels have been credited with helping to address issues that have been ignored by the national news channels (Parthasarathi and Srinivas 2012). The broadcasting industry is known to have a strong presence of corporate and political interests (Kohli-Khandekar 2012). Regional-language broadcasting appears to have a visible presence of political parties and politicians either directly or indirectly, as participants at various levels of the television industry value chain of content production, broadcasting and distribution. The Tamil-language media industry is a prime example of direct political participation in television broadcasting and other media industries.

Viewers would prefer to subscribe to only those channels that they want to view, since it allows them to pay only for those channels that they have chosen, whereas broadcasters gain from offering a bouquet of bundled channels. "What makes India a particularly sophisticated model for unbundled television is that it has 700 million TV viewers who demand accommodation for not just one, but at least 10 major languages" (Trieu 2015, 1). Bouquetisation allows less popular channels to be bundled with in-demand channels (Agnihotri 2002). This means broadcasters with popular channels can leverage their market power to control the price of the bundled channels (even if some of the channels in their bundle are not popular) and also allows the existing broadcasters to raise the barriers to entry by other broadcasters (see Nalebuff 2004).

India is being held up as an example for other countries because by law, Indian television channels need to be made available in an unbundled or à la carte form so that viewers are able to choose only the channels they want, making cable television subscriptions driven more by consumers' choices and affordable (Trieu 2015).

Scheduling strategies in multi-channel environment and the limits and problems of competitive scheduling strategies

The primary role of a broadcaster is aggregation of content. As we learnt earlier, advertising is a major revenue stream for television broadcasters in India. "The business of commercial broadcasting is the selling of audiences to advertisers—the larger the audience, the higher the commercial rates" (McDowell and Sutherland 2000, 233). Hence, content that is attractive to the demographic that the advertiser wants to target is either commissioned from independent producers or produced in house. The content can be of various genres including soap operas, sitcoms, game shows, talent contests and so on if it is a general entertainment channel.

These shows are then placed onto a 24-hour grid called a fixed point chart (FPC) based on research about the viewing habits of the demographic segments that advertisers are eager to reach. "The schedule is the locus of power in television, the mechanism whereby demographic speculations are turned into a viewing experience" (Ellis 2000, 26). The aim is to keep viewers from changing channels once they tune in (Flint 2015). "It is no secret among television executives that the best predictor of a program's audience size is usually the size of the audience leading into it" (McDowell and Sutherland 2000, 234). The best known example of scheduling to take advantage of lead in programming is when Star Plus followed *Kaun Banega Crorepati* with *Kyunki Saas Bhi Kabhi Bahu Thi* in 2000 (Sarkar 2012). Counter-programming is identified as another commonly used pattern in scheduling television programmes, where a channel schedules a programme that is different from the type playing on competing channels and is also able to attract viewers who may not be interested in what the competition is offering (Adams 1993).

The television industry in India received a later start than in many other countries, and during its early history in the second half of the 20th century it was an entirely government-operated enterprise. Today, at the beginning of the third decade of the 21st century, this vibrant system consists of both government-owned and privately owned entities that reach audiences in multiple Indian languages. Free to air, cable and satellite and direct to home are the most popular distribution systems in the country. Thus, government funding, advertising and subscription form the major revenue streams for this sector. The Ministry of Information and Broadcasting and the Telecom Regulatory Authority of India (TRAI) are the main authorities that play a regulatory role in this sector, while content is self-regulated through the News Broadcasting Standards Authority and the Indian Broadcasting Foundation. Content production, broadcasting and distribution are the three segments of the television industry. The implementation of the digital access system in distribution has served to increase the number of channels that reach audiences while simultaneously increasing the transparency of the number of users and therefore subscription revenues. Regional-language news and entertainment channels provide advertisers the opportunity to reach audiences through multiple Indian languages and are growing revenue streams in the television industry.

References

Adams, W. J. (1993). TV program scheduling strategies and their relationship to new program renewal rates and rating changes. *Journal of Broadcasting & Electronic Media*, 37(4), 465–474.

Agnihotri, A. (2002, May 16). Conditional access system: Way out of cable conundrum? Part II. *Exchange4media*. Retrieved from www.exchange4media.com/others/conditional-access-systemway-out-of-cable-conundrum-part-ii_5381.html

Annual Report 2014–15. (2015). New Delhi: Publications Division, Ministry of Information and Broadcasting, Government of India. Retrieved from mib.nic.in/writereaddata/documents/Annual_Report_2014–15.pdf

Annual Report 2015–16. (2016). New Delhi: Publications Division, Ministry of Information and Broadcasting, Government of India. Retrieved from mib.nic.in/writereaddata/documents/Annual_Report_2015–16.pdf

Annual Report 2019–20. (2020). New Delhi: Publications Division, Ministry of Information and Broadcasting, Government of India. Retrieved from https://mib.gov.in/sites/default/files/Annual%20Report%202019-20.pdf

Athique, A. M. (2009). From monopoly to polyphony: India in the era of television. In G. Turner and J. Tay (Eds.), *Television Studies after TV: Understanding Television in the Post-Broadcast Era* (pp. 159–168). New York: Routledge.

Bansal, S. (2004, November 8). You can dictate TV shows now! *Rediff.Com*. Retrieved from http://www.rediff.com/money/2004/nov/08spec2.htm?print=true

Carriage fee on a rise again? (2014, November). *IndianTelevision.com*. Retrieved from www.indiantelevision.com/cabletv/msos/carriagefeeonariseagain141118

Chris, C. (2006). Can you repeat that? Patterns of media ownership and the "repurposing" trend. *The Communication Review*, 9(1), 63–84.

DeLong, J., and Froomkin, A. (2000). Speculative microeconomics for tomorrow's economy. *First Monday*, 5(2). doi:10.5210/fm.v5i2.726

Digitise India: Carrying all pay channels in base pack holding up ARPU growth. (2016, February 10). *Televisionpost.com*. Retrieved from www.televisionpost.com/events/digitiseindiacarryingallpaychannelsinbasepackholdinguparpugrowth/

Economic Survey 2014–15. (2015). New Delhi: Ministry of Finance, Government of India. Retrieved from indiabudget.nic.in/es2014-15/echapter-vol1.pdf

Economic Survey 2015–16 (2016). New Delhi: Ministry of Finance, Government of India. Retrieved from indiabudget.nic.in/survey.asp

Ellis, J. (2000). Scheduling: The last creative act in television? *Media, Culture & Society*, 22(1), 25–38.

Flint, J. (2015, May 10). The new calculations of TV scheduling. *The Wall Street Journal*. Retrieved from www.wsj.com/articles/thenewcalculationsoftvscheduling1431250441

The Future: Now Streaming. (2016). Mumbai. Retrieved from KPMG.com/in/ficci-frames.com

Keane, M., and Moran, A. (2008). Television's new engines. *Television and New Media*, 9(2), 155–169.

Kohli-Khandekar, V. (2011, December 23). How digital cinema is changing the film business. *Business Standard*. Retrieved from www.businessstandard.com/article/printerfriendlyversion?article_id=111122300028_1

Kohli-Khandekar, V. (2012, January 31). Cinema advertising: Rising from the ashes. *Business Standard*. Retrieved from www.businessstandard.com/article/printerfriendly version?article_id=112013100005_1

Kumar, S. (2014). Media industries in India: An emerging regional framework. *Media Industries*, 1(2).

McDowell, W., and Sutherland, J. (2000). Choice versus chance: Using brand equity theory to explore TV audience lead-in effects, a case study. *The Journal of Media Economics*, 13(4), 233–247.

Nalebuff, B. (2004). Bundling as an entry barrier. *The Quarterly Journal of Economics*, 159–187.

Network 18 finishes Rs 2,053cr deal to acquire ETV stakes. (2014, January 22). *The Economic Times*. Retrieved from https://economictimes.indiatimes.com/industry/media/entertainment/media/network18-finishes-rs-2053-cr-deal-to-acquire-etv-stakes/articleshow/29215772.cms?from=mdr

Noll, R. (1993). The economics of information: A user's guide. In *The Knowledge Economy: The Nature of Information in the 21st Century*. Annual Review of the Institute for Information Studies 1993–1994. Nashville, TN: Aspen Institute and Queenstown, MD: Northern Telecom, Inc.

Parbat, K., and Nag, A. (2007, September 13). TV shows & mobile telephony set SMS turf on fire. *The Economic Times*. Retrieved from http://articles.economictimes.india times.com/20070913/news/27681080_1_smsvolumessmsrevenuemobiletelephony

Parthasarathi, V., and Srinivas, A. (2012, December 15). *Mapping Digital Media: India*. Retrieved from www.mappingdigitalmedia.org

Parthasarathi, V., and Srinivas, A. (2016, April 30). Why Indian politicians buy cable operations. *Media Power Monitor*. Retrieved from http://mediapowermonitor.com/content/why-indian-politicians-buy-cable-operations

Sarkar, A. (2012, April 30). The art of perfect timing. *AFAQS.com*. Retrieved from www.afaqs. com/news/story/33890_The-consumer-is-a-medium-Global-New-Realities-Study

Shashidhar, A. (2015, April 20). Going gets tougher for regional broadcasters as national players expand footprint. *Business Today*. Retrieved from www.businesstoday.in/storyprint/217711

Smythe, D. W. (1977). Communications: Blindspot of western marxism. *Canadian Journal of Political and Social Theory, 1*(3), 1–27.

Star India's FTA Hindi channel Utsav launching 7 June. (2004, May 18). *Indiantelevision.com*. Retrieved from www.indiantelevision.com/old-html/headlines/y2k4/may/may153.htm

Star Plus, Airtel penalised Rs 1 crore for KBC. (2008 September 11). *India Today*. Retrieved from http://indiatoday.intoday.in/story/Star+Plus+Airtel+penalised+Rs+1+crore+for+KBC/1/15107.html

Tiwari, A. K. (2013, June 10). Phase 2 digitisation spoils seen in 3–4 months. *DNA*. Retrieved from www.dnaindia.com/money/report-phase-2-digitisation-spoils-seen-in-3-4-months-1845901

TRAI puts ceiling on SMS, calls rates for TV and radio shows. (2012, April 26). *Moneylife*. Retrieved from www.moneylife.in/article/trai-puts-ceiling-on-sms-calls-rates-for-tv-and-radio-shows/25220.html

Trieu, R. (2015, February 25). How India is ahead of the game in TV unbundling. *Forbes Asia*. Retrieved from www.forbes.com/sites/rosatrieu/2015/02/25/howindiaisaheadof thegameintvunbundling/print/

Vasi, N. (2005, July 23). KBC makes Airtel a crorepati. *The Times of India*. Retrieved from http://timesofindia.indiatimes.com/india/KBCmakesAirtelacrorepati/articleshow/1180691.cms

A Year Off Script: Time for Resilience. (2020). India's Media and Entertainment Report. Retrieved from https://home.kpmg/in/en/home/insights/2020/09/media-and-entertainment-report-kpmg-india-2020-year-off-script.html

7

ECONOMICS AND MANAGEMENT OF THE FILM INDUSTRY

The film industry in India is over a century old. It has histories in multiple Indian-language markets (see Barnouw and Krishnaswamy 1980). That is, unlike many countries around the world including the biggest film markets such as the United States, France, Japan, Germany, the UK, Spain and China, India is not a monolithic market for films produced in one national language. India is a mosaic of markets in a number of languages; this puts it in a small group of countries such as Canada, Belgium and Kenya that produce films in multiple languages (Chitrapu 2012). How does this have an effect on the films available in India? We examine this question in this chapter. To do this, let us begin by familiarising ourselves with the research on the economic characteristics of film in the first section and proceed to examine the revenue streams for films in the second section. In the third section, we discuss the challenges and opportunities for the industry, including those presented by language markets. The fourth section looks at growth strategies, the star system and revenue maximisation strategies, and the last section presents current trends in the industry such as digitisation, multiplexes, FDI and overseas distribution.

Economic characteristics of film production

Before we examine the specific nuances of the economics of film industries in India, we need to familiarise ourselves with some of the economic characteristics of film production. As we all know, production, distribution and exhibition are the three activities that take place in the film industry. A single firm may participate in one or more of these activities.

As we discussed in Chapter 1, film production attracts a high first copy cost. The cost of the entire cast and crew, the special effects, the music—that is, the entire production cost is to be borne before the very first copy of the film can be

DOI: 10.4324/9781003199212-7

produced. In comparison to the first copy cost, the cost of producing subsequent copies pales into insignificance, more so in this age of digital film distribution. In order to maximise her profit, a film distributor aims to reach the largest possible audience, she does this through market segmentation and price discrimination.

Audiences vary in the value they place on a film. We know that according to the law of demand, as price falls, demand increases. There might be some *high-value* consumers who are willing to pay more to view a film and many more who might want to pay much less. Market segmentation allows film distributors to separate high-value consumers from lower-value consumers. This is done through the practice of *windowing* and *inter-temporal price discrimination* (Waterman 2005). Films are typically released at the most expensive venues first, such as multiplexes, and then over a period of time released on DVD, pay television and finally on free-to-air broadcast television. Each of these modes of release is done within in a certain window of time, and many factors influence the length of each window, including how much revenue has been earned in the previous window. Theatrical release targets the highest-value consumers, and broadcast television at the other end of the spectrum reaches the lowest-value consumers. The same film is sold to audiences but at different prices, at different venues and in different formats. This is called price discrimination. Since the film industry does this over a period of time, it is called inter-temporal price discrimination. The key to effective intertemporal price discrimination is market segmentation, the pricing of access is the method to separate high-value consumers from low-value consumers.

The unpredictability of a film's success with audiences makes risk a fundamental characteristic of film production. There is no way of knowing ahead of time whether a film will become a household name for generations like the Hindi film *Sholay* (1975; English title: *Embers*) or sink without a trace. We observe a number of practices in the film industry that arise in an attempt to mitigate risk. We discuss some of them, including the star system in a later section of this chapter and labour practices such as freelance work, at some length in a later chapter. In the next section, we examine the revenue streams in the film industry.

Revenue streams in the Indian film industry

When an Indian film is produced, the rights to its distribution through a number of different modes such as theatres, DVD, pay television and finally on free-to-air broadcast television are sold by the producer. Also since most Indian-language films are musicals, music rights also form an important revenue stream. For the producer and distributor, a film is a bundle of rights that brings in different streams of revenue. The estimates of these streams are varied. For instance, in the *Encyclopedia of Hindi Cinema*, Khanna (2003) estimates that approximately 37% of a Hindi-language film's first run revenues come from domestic theatrical distribution, approximately 18% each from overseas theatrical distribution and music rights, 12% from television broadcast rights, merchandising and product placement jointly and 2% from home video rights. Gupta (2006) estimates that 30% of a Hindi film's revenues come from the domestic box office, 25% from overseas rights, 20% from satellite broadcast rights and 10% each from music and home video. One industry report (Indywood 2016) estimates that 74% of the film industry's revenues come from domestic box office, 13% from cable and satellite rights, 7% from overseas box office and 6% from other sources. Yet another report (The Era 2020) estimates that 60% revenues are from domestic box office, 14% from overseas box office and 12% from cable and satellite rights, with 14% from other sources.

No matter what the estimates are, they all agree that domestic theatrical distribution continues to be the main source of revenue for Indian films. Theatrical distribution was well established in India by the 1920s and 1930s and the country was divided into six geographical areas for theatrical distribution, which were sub-divided into 11 territories by the beginning of the 21st century (Khanna 2003). From the late 1970s onwards, music companies started purchasing music rights outright, offering producers a revenue stream early in the production process unlike in earlier years when producers received royalties only for film music that was sold to the dominant music company HMV (Kasbekar 2006).

Satellite channels have emerged as big buyers of film broadcast rights with their demand for libraries of films of all budgets with pre-release purchase of rights that can contribute up to 35% of a film's budget (Raghavendra 2012). However, the satellite rights market is heavily dependent on the ratings that films are able to generate when telecast on cable and satellite channels (Berry 2002). Additionally, satellite rights are bought for ten-year to perpetuity periods which build channel film libraries and exert downward pressure on the prices that channels are willing to pay for films (Rao 2013)

Integrated marketing communications or product placement has emerged as popular revenue stream to Indian film producers in recent years. It offers the advantage of clutter-free celebrity brand endorsements that reach a wide audience who cannot mute them or channel surf (Kripalani 2006). Over a period of 20 years, from 1991 to 2010, the brands in Hindi films have significantly increased with Coca-Cola, Mercedes and Indian brand airlines appearing most frequently in Hindi films ranked in the top-25 box office hits in 2010 (Nelson and Deshpande 2013). Media barter, where the advertiser supports the promotion of the film on TV, in print and on hoardings, is one of the ways in which producers and distributors are compensated for product placement (Kripalani 2006).

Language dubbing, re-make rights and theatre advertising provide some additional revenues. Dubbing and re-make rights assume some importance in south Indian cinema with big-budget films (such as *Lingaa* featuring superstar Rajnikant) being released simultaneously in two or more languages in neighbouring states (Dundoo 2015).

In-theatre advertising is popular because it allows geographic segmentation and generates a captive audience (Gupta 2014). Multiplex chains offer access to high-value consumers, and consolidation in this exhibition segment has increased the ease of booking ads (Kohli-Khandekar 2012). Soft drinks and snack foods dominated the top ten advertisers in multiplexes in 2014 (Gupta 2014).

Merchandising is not a significant revenue stream in India (Udasi 2013); however, the emergence of consolidated national apparel and departmental store chains has begun to offer producers the opportunity to add some revenues through the sale of merchandise which were earlier absorbed by the unorganised sector (Sarkar and Nayak 2009).

Government certification of films is mandatory before exhibition in India. While this is not a regulation with an economic goal, it has an economic impact. As we discovered in Chapter 1, media industries enjoy economies of scale, and every media producer tries to reach the largest audience possible to maximise revenues. An "Adults Only" certificate restricts the market that a film can reach and therefore the revenue it can earn.

Challenges and opportunities for Indian film industries

Khanna (2003) presents a detailed description of the complex arrangements between Indian film producers, distributors and exhibitors, beginning with four types of contracts between producers and distributors—minimum guarantee royalty contract, outright sale contract, advance contract and commission basis contract. Under the minimum guarantee royalty contract, the producer assigns theatrical exhibition rights for a period of seven years to the distributor in return for a minimum amount of money plus print and publicity costs, before the release of the film. All these amounts plus a 20% distributor commission are deducted by the distributor from the box office earnings and the remainder, called an "overflow," is split between the distributor and producer. Big budget films made by established producers are distributed under this type of contract. Ganti (2015) points out that that the distributor bears the risk in this type of contract.

In an outright sale contract, overflows belong to the distributor and are not shared with the producer. Under the advance contract, the producer bears all the risk. All the aforementioned amounts are treated as a refundable advance from the distributor to the producer, and the producer has to refund all the amounts to the distributor within 12–18 months if they cannot be recovered from the box office earnings. In a commission basis contract, the distributor pays only for print costs and publicity and recovers these amounts along with the distributor's commission from the box office earnings. Advance and commission basis contracts are the most common type of contracts for most films.

The research on the importance given to languages in India is extensive (Mir 2006; Schiffman 1996; Laitin 1989) and one has only to see how our states are organised on the basis of language to understand the fundamental importance of languages to Indian media audiences. The economic impacts of film markets in multiple languages are many. To begin with, market size determines the budgets that are available to film producers. Larger language markets support films with larger budgets. According to the home market model of media trade (Waterman 1988; Wildman and Siwek 1988), this gives films from larger markets a competitive advantage when they are traded. We see this in the enormous popularity of Hindi-language films all over India, even in states where Hindi is not spoken by much of the population. We also see the effect of fragmented markets on the genres of films produced in the different Indian languages. While Indian films do not fit the genre categories that American films fit into, Indian films have many genre elements in them. Films produced in larger language markets have elements of expensive genres like action (Chitrapu 2012). Larger budgets are required to support action and special effects-laden films, while lower budgets are needed to produce drama and comedy films (Waterman 2005).

Cinema theatres are a state subject under Indian law; this allows Indian states to determine how they can be licenced and how theatre tickets can be priced (Khanna 2003). Theatrical exhibition attracts entertainment tax which is paid on every ticket sold. For instance in Tamil Nadu, in October 2015, the price of theatre tickets could not exceed INR 120 while "films with Tamil titles and promoting Tamil culture besides avoiding violence and bloodshed" (Don't pass entertainment tax 2015) enjoyed a 30% entertainment tax rebate which was to be passed on to the consumer. In Maharashtra, entertainment tax on cinema tickets followed a tiered system of between 45% and 54%, earning the state a revenue of INR 725 crores in 2014–2015 (Phadke 2015).

We also find that many states offer subsidies and other forms of support to films produced in their languages. In 1997, Maharashtra began to waive entertainment tax on the exhibition of Marathi-language films (Kavoori and Punathambekar 2008). Marathi film production increased after film production subsidies were introduced by the state government in 2000 (Chitrapu 2011). Screen quotas and tax rebates are also popular forms of support extended by state governments to films produced in their state languages. These measures help to mitigate the risk that is inherent in the film industry and incentivise film production in the state language. Critics of these measures argue that they reduce the film producers' incentive to make high-quality films that can compete with films in other languages.

Digital distribution of films in India began in 2003, and by 2011, two companies, Real Image (QUBE) and UFO Moviez, were the leading companies supplying the technology for digital film distribution in India to both multiplexes and single-screen theatres (Kohli-Khandekar 2011). While digital projection systems initially cost about double that of conventional projection systems, digital distribution is attractive for its ability to reduce delays in films reaching smaller towns and prevent piracy (Vidyasagar 2004). Digital distribution offers economies of scale by reaching several theatres simultaneously, prevents loss of print quality and promotes transparency at the exhibition end by preventing unauthorised screenings (Stephanie 2012). Digital distribution companies are also consolidating advertising through exhibitors, thereby reducing transaction costs and paving the way for national advertisers such as Hindustan Unilever to negotiate deals for in-theatre advertising (Kohli-Khandekar 2011).

Growth strategies of Indian film firms

A vertically integrated film company is a firm that participates in more than one of the main activities of the film industry, i.e., production, distribution and exhibition. For instance, Yash Raj Films, the film company started by the late Yash Chopra, is the producer of approximately 70 films including the cult classic *Dilwale Dulhaniya Le Jayenge* (1995) and the *Dhoom* series (2004, 2006, 2013). It is an example of a vertically integrated film company which both produces and distributes films in India and around the world.

Yash Raj Films is also a horizontally integrated company because in addition to its existing production activities, it also owns Y-Films, another production company that produces films for a youth audience. Horizontal integration remains a popular growth strategy for film production firms. From the 1980s onwards, worldwide horizontal integration deals in film production through mergers and acquisitions have exceeded those in distribution and exhibition (Jin 2012). Media firms that are both vertically and horizontally integrated are called conglomerates. Yash Raj Films is an example of a conglomerate with interests in film and television production, distribution, marketing, merchandising and various allied activities.

Horizontal and vertical integration are advantageous because of the economies of scale and scope that they offer. They also increase a firm's market power. Eventually, such a firm may dominate a market and act in an anti-competitive manner. In the Hollywood studio era of the early 20th century, the American film industry was vertically integrated, i.e., Hollywood film studios produced films, distributed them and exhibited them in their theatres. This attracted anti-trust regulation from the US government, and the Paramount case of 1947 ended this domination of the market by studios by disallowing the participation of studios involved in production and distribution in exhibition. Hollywood studios today are limited to production and distribution activities. However, they continue to be heavily horizontally integrated, using mergers and acquisitions to add production companies to their holdings (Waterman 2005).

Vertical and horizontal integration help film companies manage the risk that is inherent in the film business. Some other methods used by Hollywood film studios to mitigate risk include diversification, through the distribution of a number of different films which independent producers are not able to do, as well as through the ownership of businesses that offer steady revenues such as television channels (Waterman 2005). Along with producing films with different kinds of themes, casting star actors with a large fan base is another popular method of reducing risk (Bose 2006). With the entry of institutional capital in the form of loans from banks, completion bonds and insurance have become an important means of hedging against risk (Bose 2006). The larger film production houses, such as Eros, UTV, Reliance Entertainment, Viacom 18 Motion Pictures and Balaji Telefilms, spread their risk over a number of films and over the many ways in which a film will reach its audience including television, the rights for which are sold well before films are released for theatrical exhibition (Mahanta 2011).

The star system

Hollywood's star system is documented to have arisen from the competition in the film industry between independent producers and member companies of a group called the Motion Picture Patents Company from 1909 onwards (Kindem 1982). In the 1910s, exhibitors in America started demanding films with well-known stars as they found that these films attracted larger audiences (Kindem 1982). As we have discussed earlier in this chapter, the film industry is a risky business (De Vany and Walls 1999). One way to mitigate this risk has been to cast *stars*, who can be defined as "creatives with proven consumer appeal and high brand value" (Lorenzen 2007, 17). In fact, Albert (1998) goes so far as to suggest that, "today the power wielded by movie stars underscores much of the motion picture industry" (p. 249).

The risk mitigation offered by casting stars can be observed at three different points. As Kindem (1982) observes, the three main benefits offered by the star system are that it plays an important role in "securing and protecting production investments, differentiating movie products, and for ensuring some measure of box office success" (p. 93). Well before audiences are targeted, film production companies see stars as vital for attracting film financing (Lorenzen and Taeube 2007). Secondly, as Albert (1998) argues, "the value of stars, as a group, is partly due to their marking successful film types in a consistent, predictable way" (p. 251), i.e., they provide signals to the audience about the *type* of film that they are going to watch *before* they watch the films, much like promos and reviews that are published ahead of the film's release. In this aspect, stars show a certain "usefulness in estimating probabilities of success" (Albert 1998, 264). And finally, of course, big stars do bring in enormous revenues when compared to films made without stars (De Vany and Walls 1999; Waterman 2005; Elberse 2007).

However, when it comes to the individual film, as we all know, the presence of a star is no guarantee of that particular film being a hit and making a profit. Therefore, we should not be surprised to see research studies that argue that the presence of stars has nothing to do with a particular film's revenues (see De Vany and Walls 1999; Albert 1998).

Closer home, in Mumbai's Hindi-language film industry, Lorenzen and Taeube (2007) observe that, "a continuously replenished core group of a dozen male and a few more (and smaller) female star actors still plays a far larger role for a mainstream film's success than in the contemporary Hollywood star system" (p. 20). This brings us to one of the main economic disadvantages of the star system—the barriers to entry that it raises. The tightness of the Hindi film core network which Lorenzen and Taeube (2010) refer to as "cliquish relationships between a core of producers, directors and actors" (p. 22) is sustained by informal personal relations which raise the barriers to entry for "outsiders" including "corporate" film production companies (Lorenzen and Taeube 2007).

Revenue maximisation strategies

Waterman (2005) analyses how Hollywood film studios gained from newer means of film distribution, such as premium satellite channels including HBO, DVD sales and a variety of cable and free-to-air terrestrial broadcast channels. According to his analysis, the main contributions of these newer ways to reach audiences were market segmentation and price discrimination which separated those who were willing to pay higher amounts from those who were willing to pay lower amounts for the same film, reaching the highest-value consumers in the theatres first and then over successive windows of time, working their way down to the lowest-value consumers over terrestrial broadcast television. The earlier windows offer individual unbundled films so that greater revenues can be extracted through à la carte pricing. Later windows offer films that are bundled together through premium film channels and eventually on free-to-air broadcast channels. Each market segment was then offered the same film at a different price at a different point in time. This intertemporal price discrimination as a revenue maximisation strategy is successful when markets can be effectively segmented. Price discrimination reduces the deadweight loss that is associated with a single price.

Theatrical distribution is considered to be the best way to reach the highest-value consumer and is first in the intertemporal distribution windows. Films are released on Fridays, and the opening weekend is the time when the greatest revenues can be earned (Dixon 2012). This is because, traditionally, distributors' share of the box office revenues are negotiated to be the highest in the earliest days of theatrical release (Marich 2005). This is known as "front-loading" (Squire 2006). Distributors would like to maximise these revenues through "wide releases," i.e. releasing the film in multiple theatres simultaneously. In India especially, wide releases help combat piracy (Ganti 2013).

In the United States, the purchase of home video formats including VHS and DVD is driven by "just three words: kids, collections, and gifts" (Waterman 2005, 88). Repetitive viewing by children, collections by fans and popularity as Christmas gifts are all seen as contributing to film studio revenues from home video formats. While home video is not considered to be a viable revenue stream in India due to losses through piracy, satellite and music rights are seen as reliable revenue streams.

While windows are well thought out and planned in advance to avoid cannibalising on revenues, occasionally we see a clash between different rights holders. When satellite television began to emerge as a lucrative opportunity, Indian film producers began selling satellite rights to television channels that were eager to exploit them, putting them on a collision course with distributors who held theatrical distribution rights and were hoping to recover their investment through releases in smaller towns over a period of time; this is because unlike in Hollywood, where studios integrate production and distribution, the Indian film industry has separate firms in film production and distribution (Ganti 2013).

Language dubbing of films offers an additional revenue stream in India to film distributors of both Hollywood and Indian-language films that have been dubbed into different Indian languages for theatrical exhibition. They are also popular on television channels. However, in some states, the exhibition of language-dubbed films has been opposed on the grounds that it poses a threat not only to the livelihood of film workers in those states but also to the culture of those states. In 2018, in the case of G. *Krishnamurthy v. Karnataka Film Chamber of Commerce (KFCC) and others*, Case No. 42 of 2017, the Competition Commission of India held that such opposition was an anti-competitive practice that negatively impacted distributor revenues as well as the choice available to consumers.

Trends

Digitisation

In India, digital distribution of films to theatres via satellite eliminates physical film prints and allows simultaneous wide release over a wide geographical area. This reduces print costs and acts as a deterrent to piracy (Ganti 2013). The growth of digital cable and satellite distribution internationally has meant that audiences are now accessed through "addressable" systems that can be controlled on the basis of payments made by individual consumers (Waterman 2005). Compare this with the "free" access that terrestrial broadcast television once offered audiences, and it immediately becomes clear why global entertainment firms have thrown their weight behind digitisation. Music rights which were exploited through cassette sales in the previous century are now digitally exploited through streaming audio services and as ringtones. Punathambekar (2013) argues that the interactions that the Hindi film industry has had with television and digital media industries have played an important role in its recent growth both within and outside India.

Multiplexes

Multiplexes offer yet another opportunity for market segmentation. In 2019, India was estimated to have approximately 9,527 theatrical screens of which 34% (3,200 screens) were multiplex screens and the remaining 66% (6,327 screens) were single screens. By 2019, the multiplex business was highly consolidated, with five companies—PVR Cinemas (812 screens), Inox Leisure (612 screens), Carnival Cinemas (450 screens), Cinepolis India (381 screens) and Miraj (125 screens)—accounting for 74% of the screens (The Era 2020). Theatrical audiences can now be thought of in two distinct segments—single-screen audiences and multiplex audiences. These theatrical exhibition venues reach high-value consumers who are willing to pay premium ticket prices for superior-quality film consumption experience in a luxurious ambience. In addition to the entertainment they offer on their screens, multiplexes, through their ticket price wars, provide a fascinating opportunity to students interested in the intersection of media economics, public policy and culture. Ticket pricing in multiplexes is a contentious issue. For instance, the government of the state of Karnataka, like its neighbouring states Tamil Nadu and Telangana, imposed a ceiling on multiplex ticket prices to promote Kannada-language films which are exhibited to a lesser extent in the multiplexes compared to their expensively produced competitors in other languages (Poovanna 2017). However, this price ceiling was struck down for weekends, when theatre occupancy is highest, through an interim order of the High Court of Karnataka (Express News Service 2017). Two years later, as of this writing, the matter was still pending in court with calls from the Karnataka Film Chamber of Commerce to implement the price ceiling (Khajane 2019) Despite early conflicts with film producers and distributors, as we have seen from the section on competition policy in India, consolidated multiplex chains including PVR, Inox and Fame, which are aided by tax rebates from governments, offer lower transaction costs to distributors as well as in-theatre advertising revenues. We now see the production of "multiplex films," a genre of films which cater to an upper-middle-class demographic as opposed to films aimed at single-screen audiences.

FDI

Government policy placed several restrictions on Hollywood imports into India for many decades due to a shortage of foreign exchange (Pendakur 1985). These restrictions were lifted after the opening of India's markets in the 1990s, and 100% foreign direct investment (FDI) is now allowed in all areas of the film industry in India (Ganti 2013). However, Indian film audiences have a strong preference for domestic film productions. Hollywood studios have had to resort to co-productions with Indian film producers as a strategy to reach Indian film audiences (Rasul and Proffitt 2012). Hollywood studios including Disney (which acquired Indian film and television firm UTV in a much-publicised deal), Viacom and Fox have a presence in the Mumbai film industry. In a reverse flow of investment, Reliance Entertainment owns a 50% stake in the Hollywood studio DreamWorks (Punathambekar 2013). In 2015, a film facilitation office was set up under the Make in India initiative to streamline permissions for film shooting in India.

Overseas distribution

Until the first decade of the 21st century, overseas markets for Indian films were restricted to countries where there was an Indian diaspora and markets in Africa and Eastern Europe where they enjoyed cultural proximity and an economic advantage over domestic productions (Chitrapu 2012). However in the second decade of this century, spurred by increased revenues from domestic demand, this began to change. As Ganti (2013) points out, international distribution rights which were originally sold for a single "overseas" territory are now divided into several geographic territories including North America, the United Kingdom, the Gulf States and South Africa. In addition to overseas theatrical revenues, home video is now thought to provide a reliable revenue stream for Indian distribution companies, such as Eros International, which have a presence in the American and British markets (Punathambekar 2013). In 2019, 350 Indian films found an international theatrical release, and the region-wise breakup is estimated to be China (31%), USA/Canada 23%, Gulf 19%, UK 6%, Australia 4% and other regions 16% (The Era 2020). In 2010, *My Name Is Khan* was reported to have been distributed in 30 countries (UNESCO 2013). Annual reports of international distributors of Indian films such as Eros list their markets to include Germany, Poland, Russia, France, Italy, Spain, Indonesia, Malaysia, Japan, South Korea, China, the Middle East and Latin America (Eros 2020).

India presents a unique mosaic of many language film markets unlike other film-producing countries. Language plays a very important role in determining the structure of Indian film markets. While privately owned firms produce, distribute and exhibit films, both the central and state governments shape Indian-language film markets. Films are certified by the Central Board of Film Certification, a central government body. State governments play an important role in their language film industries, from imposing price ceilings on ticket prices to providing subsidies for film production in the state language. The production, distribution and exhibition segments in Indian-language film markets show the presence of both vertically and horizontally integrated firms. The main revenue streams are domestic theatrical distribution followed by cable and satellite rights. The emergence of multiplexes to cater to high-value consumers allows for sharper market segmentation in domestic theatrical exhibition. Overseas distribution is an emerging source of revenue in recent decades.

References

Albert, S. (1998). Movie stars and the distribution of financially successful films in the motion picture industry. *Journal of Cultural Economics*, *22*(4), 249–270. Retrieved from www.jstor.org.proxyiub.uits.iu.edu/stable/41810673

Barnouw, E., and Krishnaswamy, S. (1980). *Indian Film* (2nd ed.). New York: Oxford University Press.

Berry, S. (2002, May 1). Plunge pool. *Television Asia*. Retrieved from http://bi.galegroup.com.proxyiub.uits.iu.edu/essentials/article/GALE%7CA86867087/a70e16ea1483a02fe030f83aab24055b?u=iuclassb

Bose, D. (2006). *Brand Bollywood: A New Global Entertainment Order*. New Delhi, India: Sage Publications.

Chitrapu, S. (2011). *The Political Economy of Indian Language Film Production: The Case of Marathi Cinema*. Paper presented at the 20th Annual Conference of the Asian Media Information and Communication Centre (AMIC), Hyderabad, India.

Chitrapu, S. (2012). A regional mosaic: Linguistic diversity and India's film trade. In A. G. Roy (Ed.), *The Magic of Bollywood: At Home and Abroad* (pp. 81–106). New Delhi: Sage Publications.

De Vany, A., and Walls, W. D. (1999). Uncertainty in the movie industry: Does star power reduce the terror of the box office? *Journal of Cultural Economics, 23*(4), 285–318. Retrieved from www.jstor.org.proxyiub.uits.iu.edu/stable/41810703

Dixon, W. W. (2012). *Death of the Moguls: The End of Classical Hollywood*. New Brunswick: Rutgers University Press.

Don't pass entertainment tax on to viewers: Madras High Court tells theatre owners. (2015, October 30). *DNA*. Retrieved from www.dnaindia.com/entertainment/report-don-t-pass-entertainment-tax-on-to-viewers-madras-high-court-tells-theatre-owners-2140146

Dundoo, S. D. (2015, May 17). The curious case of dubbed films. *The Hindu*. Retrieved from www.thehindu.com/features/metroplus/the-curious-case-of-dubbed-films/article7214084.ece?css=print

Elberse, A. (2007). The power of stars: Do star actors drive the success of movies? *Journal of Marketing, 71*(4), 102–120. Retrieved from www.jstor.org.proxyiub.uits.iu.edu/stable/30164000

The Era of Consumer ART: Acquisition, Retention, Transaction. (2020). Federation of Indian Chambers of Commerce and Industry (FICCI) and EY India.

Eros International Plc. (2020). *2020 SEC Filing Form 20-F*. Retrieved from https://erosstx.gcs-web.com/sec-filings/sec-filing/20-f/0001171520-20-000426

Express News Service. (2017, May 12). Karnataka HC strikes down govt order: No Rs 200 cap on movie tickets on weekends, holidays. *The New Indian Express*. Retrieved from www.newindianexpress.com/states/karnataka/2017/may/12/karnataka-hc-strikes-down-govt-order-no-rs-200-cap-on-movie-tickets-on-weekends-holidays-1603911.html

Ganti, T. (2013). *Bollywood: A Guidebook to Popular Hindi Cinema*. Abingdon, UK: Routledge.

Ganti, T. (2015). Fuzzy numbers: The productive nature of ambiguity in the Hindi film industry. *Comparative Studies of South Asia, Africa and the Middle East* (3), 451. Retrieved from http://proxyiub.uits.iu.edu/login?url=http://search.ebscohost.com/login.aspx?direct=true&db=edspmu&AN=edspmu.S1548226X15300069&site=eds-live&scope=site

G. Krishnamurthy v. Karnataka Film Chamber of Commerce (KFCC) and Others (Case 42/2017). (2018). Competition Commission of India. Retrieved from www.cci.gov.in/sites/default/files/Case%20No%2042%20of%202017.pdf

Gupta, S. D. (2006, May 27). How Bollywood makes money. *Rediff.com*. Retrieved from www.rediff.com/money/2006/may/27spec1.htm?print=true

Gupta, S. D. (2014, August 22). In-cinema advertising takes off. *Afaqs!* Retrieved from www.afaqs.com/news/story/41704_In-Cinema-Advertising-takes-off

Indywood: The Indian Film Industry. (2016). Deloitte India. Retrieved from www2.deloitte.com/content/dam/Deloitte/in/Documents/technology-media-telecommunications/in-tmt-indywood-film-festival-noexp.pdf

Jin, D. Y. (2012). Transforming the global film industries: Horizontal integration and vertical concentration amid neoliberal globalization. *International Communication Gazette, 74*(5), 405–422. doi:10.1177/1748048512445149

Kasbekar, A. (2006). *Pop Culture India!: Media, Arts, and Lifestyle*. ABC-CLIO.

Kavoori, A. P., and Punathambekar, A. (2008). *Global Bollywood*. New York: New York University Press.

Khajane, M. (2019, February 6). In Karnataka, cap on ticket rates in multiplexes remains a distant dream. *The Hindu*. Retrieved from www.thehindu.com/news/national/kar nataka/in-karnataka-cap-on-ticket-rates-in-multiplexes-remains-a-distant-dream/ article26188020.ece

Khanna, A. (2003). The business of Hindi films. In G. Gulzar Nihalani and S. Chat-terjee (Eds.), *Encyclopaedia of Hindi Cinema* (pp. 135–154). New Delhi: Encyclopaedia Britannica.

Kindem, G. (1982). Hollywood's movie star system: A historical overview. In G. Kindem (Ed.), *The American Movie Industry: The Business of Motion Pictures* (pp. 79–93). Carbon-dale, IL: Southern Illinois University Press.

Kohli-Khandekar, V. (2011, December 23). How digital cinema is changing the film business. *Business Standard*. Retrieved from www.businessstandard.com/article/printerfriendlyversion?article_id=111122300028_1

Kohli-Khandekar, V. (2012, January 31). Cinema advertising: Rising from the ashes. *Business Standard*. Retrieved from www.businessstandard.com/article/printerfriendly version?article_id=112013100005_1

Kripalani, C. (2006). Trendsetting and product placement in Bollywood film: Con-sumerism through consumption. *New Cinemas: Journal of Contemporary Film*, 4(3), 197–215. doi:10.1386/ncin.4.3.197_1

Laitin, D. D. (1989). Language policy and political strategy in India. *Policy Sciences*, 22(3/4), 415–436. Retrieved from www.jstor.org/stable/4532177

Lorenzen, M. (2007). *Creative Encounters in the Film Industry: Content, Cost, Chance, and Collection*.

Lorenzen, M., and Taeube, F. A. (2007). *Breakout from Bollywood? Internationalization of Indian Film Industry*. Paper presented at the DRUID Working Paper No. 07-06.

Lorenzen, M., and Taeube, F. A. (2010). *The Banyan and the Birch Tree: Family Ties and Embeddedness in the Indian Film Industry in Bollywood*. Paper presented at the Creative Encounters Working Paper #40.

Mahanta, V. (2011, August 6). How Bollywood economy has changed over the past decade. *The Economic Times*. Retrieved from https://economictimes.indiatimes.com/ industry/media/entertainment/how-bollywood-economy-has-changed-over-the-past-decade/articleshow/9501682.cms

Marich, R. (2005). *Marketing to Moviegoers: A Handbook of Strategies Used by Major Studios and Independents*. Taylor and Francis.

Mir, F. (2006). Imperial policy, provincial practices: Colonial language policy in nineteenth-century India. *Indian Economic & Social History Review*, 43(4), 395–426.

Nelson, M. R., and Deshpande, S. (2013). The prevalence of and consumer response to foreign and domestic brand placement in Bollywood movies. *Journal of Advertising*, 42(1), 1–15. doi:10.1080/00913367.2012.749195

Pendakur, M. (1985). Dynamics of cultural policy making: The U.S. film industry in India. *Journal of Communication*, 35(4), 52–72.

Phadke, M. (2015, December 4). Maharashtra tourism dept mulls tax exemption on tickets if movie is shot in state. *Indian Express*. Retrieved from http://indianexpress.com/arti cle/india/indianewsindia/maharashtratourismdeptmullstaxexemptiononticketsifmovieis shotinstate/99/print/

Poovanna, S. (2017, May 2). Karnataka government caps movie ticket prices at Rs200. *Mint*. Retrieved from www.livemint.com/Politics/8nOjoZUBk2qPFrZwqgNjIO/ Karnataka-government-caps-movie-ticket-prices-at-Rs200.html

Punathambekar, A. (2013). *From Bombay to Bollywood the Making of a Global Media Industry.* New York: New York University Press.

Raghavendra, N. (2012, August 10). Satellite rights of over 100 small budget films released since 2011 unsold. *The Economic Times.* Retrieved from http://articles.economictimes.indiatimes.com/20120810/news/33137552_1_satelliterightshirengadahindifilms

Rao, S. (2013, December 17). No takers for satellite rights of many Telugu films. *The Times of India.* Retrieved from http://timesofindia.indiatimes.com/entertainment/telugu/movies/news/No-takers-for-satellite-rights-of-many-Telugu-films/articleshow/27473128.cms

Rasul, A., and Proffitt, J. M. (2012). An irresistible market: A critical analysis of Hollywood: Bollywood coproductions. *Communication, Culture & Critique, 5*(4), 563–583. Retrieved from http://proxyiub.uits.iu.edu/login?url=http://search.ebscohost.com/login.aspx?direct=true&db=mzh&AN=2013296491&site=eds-live&scope=site

Sarkar, S., and Nayak, A. (2009). Film merchandising in India. *Globsyn Management Journal, 3*(1), 1–10. Retrieved from http://proxyiub.uits.iu.edu/login?url=http://search.ebscohost.com/login.aspx?direct=true&db=buh&AN=45828224&site=eds-live&scope=site

Schiffman, H. F. (1996). *Linguistic Culture and Language Policy.* New York: Routledge.

Squire, J. E. (2006). *The Movie Business Book.* Open University Press.

Stephanie, L., Sharma, R. S., and Ramasubbu, N. (2012). The digitisation of Bollywood adapting to disruptive innovation. *Media Asia (Asian Media Information & Communication Centre), 39*(1), 3. Retrieved from http://proxyiub.uits.iu.edu/login?url=http://search.ebscohost.com/login.aspx?direct=true&db=edb&AN=86873652&site=eds-live&scope=site

Udasi, H. (2013, October 29). Movies and merchandise. *The Hindu.* Retrieved from www.thehindu.com/features/metroplus/fashion/moviesandmerchandise/article5285841.ece?css=print

UNESCO Institute for Statistics. (2013). *Emerging Markets and the Digitalization of the Film Industry: An Analysis of the 2012 UIS International Survey of Feature Film Statistics.* Information Paper No. 14. UNESCO Institute for Statistics. Retrieved from http://uis.unesco.org/sites/default/files/documents/emerging-markets-and-the-digitalization-of-the-film-industry-en_0.pdf

Vidyasagar, N. (2004). Film industry dreams in digital. *The Times of India.* Retrieved from http://timesofindia.indiatimes.com/business/indiabusiness/Filmindustrydreamsindigital/articleshowprint/484017.cms

Waterman, D. (1988). World television trade: The economic effects of privatization and new technology. *Telecommunications Policy, 12*(2), 141–151.

Waterman, D. (2005). *Hollywood's Road to Riches.* Cambridge, MA: Harvard University Press.

Wildman, S. S., and Siwek, S. E. (1988). *International Trade in Films and Television Programs.* Cambridge: Ballinger Publishing Company.

8

ECONOMICS AND MANAGEMENT OF DIGITAL MEDIA

What is digital media or new media? How is it different from older forms of media? Will it displace older forms of media? Is it a medium of creation or a medium of distribution? What business models work for content companies in digital space? These are some of the important questions to be answered in understanding what is being referred to as new media or digital media. Throughout this chapter, the authors prefer to use the words "digital media" to refer to these evolving media technologies, devices, delivery platforms and business models.

Understanding digital media markets

Digital media is a result of a variety of Internet and web technologies that came into existence in the 1990s and in the first two decades of the millennium. The important characteristic of digital media vis-à-vis analogue media is the possibility to break the information into bits and bytes. The digital data can then be stored, compressed, retrieved, repurposed and transmitted easily. The second important characteristic of digital media is the possibility of distribution through online networks. These two developments brought in synergies for hitherto different fields—media, telecom, IT and consumer electronics—and it is being referred to as convergence.

From a media economics and management point of view, the economies of scale and scope for media content can be achieved to their full potential using digital technologies. Marginal costs in digital media technologies are minimal to nil, providing it with unprecedented scale benefits as output expands. Digital content is highly suitable for repurposing. This feature enables it to be distributed across platforms and on demand, providing it with scope benefits. The multiple streams of revenues from repurposed content sold on diversified platforms will help in reducing the financial risk faced by content firms.

DOI: 10.4324/9781003199212-8

Besides scale and scope benefits, digital media also benefit from what is being referred to as "network effects." This refers to the value a new subscriber brings to the existing subscribers. A product or service possesses network effects if the utility one derives from it is a positive function of the number of other people who consume it. On the converse, as more and more subscribers start leaving the network, the value for the existing consumers reduces. Telephone is one of the oldest examples. Most media and communication technologies such as satellite and cable TV, mobile TV and IPTV are network goods in this sense: They literally constitute a network, and the value of the network depends on the number of people connected to it (Zvezdan 2009, 84). The value of being part of the network increases as the size of the network increases and decreases as the network decreases. The network effects are highly positive to already large global corporations. Many Web 2.0 services, including Skype, Facebook and Twitter, enjoy network effects. The gaming industry also enjoys network effects. Of late, traditional landline telcos are suffering from negative network effects.

Interactivity and personalisation are two important features of new media (Doyle 2002). Digital media hosted on computer servers responds to user actions in ways not possible with analogue media. The user inputs also become important in the digital media experience. Simple examples of interactivity can be the interactive programming guide (IPG) in broadcast service or graphical user interface (GUI) on our computer and mobile devices. More complex forms of interactivity can be seen in online gaming in which geographically distributed users interact with a media application. Many more interactive possibilities, including Virtual Reality (VR), are in development and commercialisation stages, but the important point to be noted is that digitisation makes it possible.

The 20th century produced audiences who were massive, passive, anonymous and heterogeneous, assembled largely for advertisers to sell their goods and services (Pavlik 2008, 221). Digital technologies allow moving away from this mass circulation and broadcasting models to narrow casting models. Digital technologies are supposed to help firms shift their focus from mass production to mass personalisation. For instance, the mainstream broadcaster's schedule is too rigid from the consumer's point of view, while the same content when provided online becomes on demand and can be self-scheduled according to their convenience. Advertisers, the key stakeholders in media business, are very keen on personalisation as it enables them to indulge in selective marketing and behavioural targeting. Personalisation also enables firms to move away from product-centred marketing to customer-centred relationship marketing. All these business strategies are being built on the advancements in digital technologies.

Will digital media displace old media?

The theoretical proposition that new and digital media will displace old forms of media is not supported by empirical evidence on ground. The newer forms of media are being consumed along with older forms of media, suggesting rising consumption of both new and incumbent media as a whole. For media firms, the question is not of displacement but of saturation and supplementation (Newell et al. 2008, 131). Book and newspaper publishing survived many new technologies, including cinema, radio, TV and now Internet by adapting to the changed environment. The evolution of digital convergence has blurred many product and geographical boundaries. All old forms of media are being made available in digital formats and across a range of digital devices. As long as publishing, film, TV and music industries can access audiences migrating from traditional delivery platforms to digital delivery platforms, they remain well off. Adapting to the new delivery platform with new business models is a challenge, but it does not amount to getting displaced. Digital media technologies have in some ways altered the existing relationship between the firms, audiences and advertisers. These new sets of relationships have in turn affected the structure of specific media industries and markets.

Old media firms will not sit idle and let the new opportunities pass by. They are often keen to adapt to new innovations. However, the adaptation depends on environmental factors (structure of the industry, competition, earlier experience of adaptations) and the firm's internal resources (HR, Systems). For instance, digital devices like set top boxes have expanded the possibility of watching 200 channels on television sets to thousands. Even though DTH providers introduced set top box services first, cable companies too adopted the technology to ensure that their consumers do not migrate to DTH. Digital distribution technologies disrupted the music market very badly. But in the last few years digital distribution has become the prime source of revenues for the music industry. Currently around 77% of revenues for the music industry in India come from digital media channels, while physical sales contribute to just 7% (*Economic Impact of the Recorded Music Industry in India 2019*, 11). Advertising and subscriptions from music streaming are principal contributors of digital revenues. Mobile companies have launched apps and streaming services to provide digital music. Audio OTT streaming is picking up. The digital technologies have increased the touch points for the music industry significantly. They have also erased the boundaries between different forms of distribution that set different media apart till recently.

Digital technologies and media distribution

Internet is by far the most prolific distribution channel that the media industry has ever had. Whether online or offline, the distribution stage of media industries has been revolutionised with the arrival of digital technologies. The productivity gains in the distribution stage have gained immensely with the arrival of digital media technologies. Meanwhile, traditional media distributors were challenged in many ways across all media segments. Telecom giants like AT&T, MCI and Verizon and Internet majors like Google and Yahoo entered content distribution, forcing traditional content distributors to adapt new strategies (Pavlik 2008, 134).

The first phase of media business on Internet started with electronic retailing by players like Amazon. They could sell books, CDs and DVDs to vast numbers of people and reap the benefits of economies of scale. Internet became one more channel of distribution for the old media products in physical format with superior inventory management. As media goods are intangible, it makes economic sense to distribute them online in non-physical form. Online distribution will reduce marginal costs and increase the profit margins. As entrepreneurs started focusing on this aspect, many on-demand services started online. The music industry was the first to adapt to digital media technologies, followed by book publishers, film producers and TV broadcasters.

After the Napster episode and the crisis in the music industry, there were many attempts to find a business model for digital music distribution. Apple came up with iTunes Music Store, a legally acceptable distribution mechanism for digital music in 2003. This new division brought in synergies with their device business, iPod. Later, iTunes store was developed into a one-stop shop for media consumption on a range of Apple devices. Soon it became the e-commerce engine for Apple by expanding its portfolio from music to movies, TV shows, books and apps. The beleaguered music industry majors were too glad to have a web model in place, and they willingly partnered with Apple in developing a giant music retailer and eventually got locked in. Even though Real Networks Inc (formerly Progressive Networks) was the first to bring audio compression and packet streaming technologies to the marketplace in 1995, it did not succeed as much. Apple was able to provide the right value proposition to the consumers with 99-cent à la carte pricing for downloading singles, while Real Networks was providing only subscription-based streaming services. The ownership of the downloaded music and the portability of iPod have contributed for its success. From the very beginning, iTunes partnered with all the big five music majors offering a 2,00,000-song library, making it a one-stop shop for music. However, in the last few years revenues from streaming music have been surging ahead, while download revenues have been coming down. International Federation of the Phonographic Industry's (IFPI) Global Music Report states that the combined ad-supported and subscription streaming revenues now account for 56.1% of global music revenues, followed by physical sales at 21.6%, performance rights at 12.6% and downloads and other digital at 7.2% respectively (Global Music Report 2020, 6).

The emergence of successful business models in digital music encouraged film and broadcast companies to foray into digital space. Launched in 2005, YouTube became a success within a year and was acquired by Google. After a few copyright infringement tussles with media companies, it entered into an agreement with MGM, CBS and Lions Gate Entertainment to host advertiser-supported films and TV episodes in 2008. With increasing Internet penetration and mobile connectivity, young viewership for streamed video on demand has been increasing globally. YouTube has been the global leader in the online video market since 2008. The user base, which is not possible for a linear traditional broadcaster, allows it to charge premium rates from the advertisers. From being an aggregator of user-generated content, it became a distribution platform for original content creators. It grew by roping in content partners for providing premium content with The Orchard Partnership. It also transformed into a live streaming platform for many events globally.

The digital video space has also seen the rise of intermediaries, who are being referred to as multi-channel networks (MCNs). These intermediaries produce content and do rights management on others' behalf. They help independent content creators distribute their video across channels ranging from YouTube, Facebook and Twitter. Big aggregators like YouTube are encouraging MCNs to bring in fresh content and to compete with the traditional content companies. All those small content companies, who could not own their broadcast network, can now easily own an MCN. MakerGen, an MCN, is behind the popular YouTube channels AIB, and East India Comedy. Its parent Maker Studios was acquired by Disney in 2016 for a fancy price. Culture Machine Media Pvt Ltd has many YouTube channels including Being Indian, SNG Comedy and Put Chutney. Many MCNs, including HomeVeda, One Digital, Nirvana Digital, One Digital, Pepper Media, Rajashri Media and Qyuki, were launched in India with backing from venture capitalists. Whether they can redefine content has to be seen over time. As of this writing, they were still trying to produce viral videos that can get them recognised, increase subscribers and thereby gain market share.

Traditional content producers and distributors are being forced to be available on digital platforms to cater to the migrating audiences. The owners of traditional media across the world have focused on launching and acquiring digital media properties in the last two decades. Digital video platforms—Hotstar, Eros Now, Box TV, Ditto TV and SonyLIV—were launched by leading content providers Star TV, Eros International, Times of India, Zee Group and Sony respectively. Most of the big DTH providers have started entering into digital video distribution online. Dish Online from Zee group, PocketTV from Airtel, EveryWhere TV from Tata Sky and Direct2Mobile by Videocon have launched their online video distribution on a monthly subscription basis.

Many established media providers acquired the requisite technology or entered into partnerships with aggregators to make on-demand provision for their customers. In 2015 five major Japanese broadcasters together launched a free online video platform named TVer, where they made their top ten programs available for a week after broadcast. It became very popular with millions of app downloads in a month's time. Such services are being launched to reach out to the younger generation who are spending more time on smartphones than on TV (Japantimes.co.jp). Cable television distributors responded to these developments by launching video programme distribution services to websites. Audiences will be able to watch streaming content as long as they watch embedded commercials. The revenues made this way are distributed between content owner, website owner and online distributor. Some popular commercial online broadcast networks in India include WhereverTV, NowTV, and YuppTV. They provide both subscription services and pay-as-you-go options to users.

The traditional media companies have been late to digital distribution. The technology majors, with their hardware, software and in some cases delivery devices, emerged as major online distributors of media content. The expansion of digital media depends on Internet bandwidth and mobile connectivity. With increasing congestion in wired networks, Internet penetration in countries like India is being driven by 3G and 4G mobile services. The proliferation of affordable smartphones in India is an indicator of the growth in this sector. India is the second largest and fastest-growing smartphone market in the world (Shooting for the Stars 2015).

Social media is purely an outcome of Internet and web technologies and therefore qualifies as digital-only media. Its ability to integrate text, pictures, music and video has only increased the demand for traditional media content. Social media penetration in India has increase significantly in the last five years, with the increasing amount of time spent on social media sites, and the young profile of the users is attracting the attention of advertisers. Social media platforms are trying to grow by introducing specialised services to the Indian users.

WhatsApp with 400 million users, Telegram with 300 million users, YouTube with 265 million users and Facebook with around 260 million users are the most popular social media service providers among Indian users. Social media activity generally peaks around sporting events, elections, movie releases and other important news developments. Advertisers are able to cash in on this by producing promotional content that works well with the event. The potential for content discovery and referral through sharing is high in social media, making it an attractive promotional vehicle for media content firms. Social media is also emerging as a content distribution channel besides being a marketing tool.

The rise of OTTs

Over-the-top platforms (OTTs) have emerged as the most successful digital platforms among all other digital media initiatives in the last decade. OTTs deliver audiovisual content through Internet via a process known as streaming. The *Global Entertainment and Media Outlook* (2020–2024) by PriceWaterhouseCoopers (PwC) states that the Indian OTT video market is the fastest growing in the world at a CAGR of 28.6% in the forecast period. The revenue models of OTTs are advertising video on demand (AVOD), subscription video on demand (SVOD), Freemium and transactional video on demand (TVOD). The AVOD and SVOD models are merged together to form the Freemium model, where some content is available free with advertisements while the rest is paywalled. The TVOD model allows consumers to pay only for the video they choose. Audio OTT platforms such as Spotify and JioSaavn have a Freemium model. Video OTT platforms like Amazon Prime Video and Netflix have an SVOD model, while SonyLIV, Zee5, and Disney+Hotstar have a freemium model.

Tech giants like Google, Apple, Amazon and Facebook have faced little regulation in terms of competition laws disallowing monopolistic behaviour and market concentration. Their superior digital infrastructure allows them to collect more data about the tastes and preferences of consumers and to personalise media content recommendations for them. This lucrative business opportunity has facilitated the entry of the tech giants into the OTT space (Fitzgerald 2019, 89–91). Netflix, on the other hand, is an OTT platform and production company that is counted amongst the Tech giants because of its high-quality content recommendation algorithm and user experience. When Netflix rolled out its service in 130 countries in early 2016, Amazon followed by launching Amazon Prime Video in 200 countries in late 2016. These international platforms have been trying to gain an edge by investing heavily in the production of original content (Fitzgerald 2019, 91–92).

There has been a lot of concentration in the OTT video space in India, with Disney+Hotstar, Amazon Prime Video and Netflix accounting for a huge portion of the paid subscriber population. The OTT, Hotstar, was rebranded as Disney+Hotstar in India in April 2020, following the acquisition of 21st Century Fox by The Walt Disney Company in 2019. This is indicative of the consolidation not only of the tech giants, but also of large traditional media companies. Disney rebranded Hotstar and diagonally expanded into the streaming space. Indian OTT video players like Zee5 and Voot, amongst others, offer catch up TV alongside acquired content and original productions.

The Indian OTT video market is distinctive because of the heterogeneous population of consumers who speak different languages. With growing rural Internet penetration, cheap mobile data prices and the growing use of smartphones, a large segment of OTT users in India prefer content in their own languages (languages other than English and Hindi). The theory of resource partitioning states that an industry could witness simultaneous trends of increased concentration and specialist proliferation under certain conditions (Carroll et al. 2002, 1–3). This explains the phenomenon of the rise of OTT platforms in regional languages. Original content is the differentiating feature of OTT platforms (Unravelling the digital video consumer 2019, September 7), and while Amazon Prime Video and Disney+Hotstar are investing in producing original content in languages besides English and Hindi, the witnessed demand is much higher. This has led to the rise of domestic OTT platforms with language-specific content.

Hoichoi, a Bengali OTT platform launched in 2017, was one of the first movers in this space. Besides the Bengali-speaking population in India, it concentrates on marketing content to the Bengali-speaking diaspora as well. Diasporic subscriptions provide domestic OTTs with higher ARPUs. Manorama Max was launched in 2019 and focuses on Malayalam content. Aha (Telugu), Talkies (Tulu, Kannada, Konkani) and Planet Marathi (Marathi) were all launched in 2020. There are around 40 OTTs in India, and experts believe that there will be increasing consolidation over the next few years because of market dynamics.

Media ecology, according to Neil Postman (2000, 10–11), studies the technology in which a culture evolves and shapes the political and social organisation. How has the rise of OTTs changed the ways in which human beings interact with this new media? The consumption of content in a binge-watching mode has changed the pattern of leisure. OTTs in general allow for temporal and spatial flexibility in consumption; binge-watching is an extension of this flexibility. The content on OTTs has shaped both popular culture and public discourse on legal and moral issues in India.

The COVID-19 pandemic hastened the rollout of several platforms and better technological features, such as the addition of Dolby core technologies on the OTTs. The pandemic caused OTTs to reinvent themselves. With the closure of public cinema halls during the COVID-19 pandemic, the gap between theatrical and streaming releases disappeared, as some movies were released direct to OTT. The lockdown periods during the pandemic, with measures such as social distancing, saw people confined to their homes. Groups of friends and families used web extensions like Teleparty (earlier Netflix Party) to sync video and chat across their separate accounts, as a reimagined way of spending time together.

Revenue strategies for content providers in the digital media space

One of the important decisions to be taken by media firms when they go online is to decide whether they will exercise pricing option, advertising option or both. Research studies suggest that media firms should sell their content online, when their content quality is relatively higher and when online access costs are low (Fan et al. 2007, 144). In markets, where access costs are higher, it makes sense for media providers to focus on advertising revenues. They can provide free content with commercial advertisements. If the access costs are low with good-quality content, then commercial-free content can be provided on a pay basis. Overall, media producers can maximise their revenues by providing both advertising and subscription options to their consumers in the digital space.

Once content firms choose either of the two options, they will also have to figure out the optimal pricing levels for advertising or content and the factors that affect those levels (Fan et al. 2007, 145). If the content quality is high, and if the digital window is mature enough, the possibilities of extracting consumer surplus will be high in this window. However, the range of content being offered and the ease of payment will also have a bearing on transactions in this distribution channel. Big aggregators with differentiated content are well suited for distributing paid content online. Online media companies like iTunes, which are into selling content and services in large quantities, have been very successful. Premium Media can be made available on demand on an à la carte or subscription basis. Instant gratification is a click away in the networked world, and this feature allows extracting consumer surplus. YouTube launched its monthly paid subscription services YouTube Originals in 2016, and YouTube Premium in

2018 after rebranding its earlier paid subscription service YouTube Red. Sporting events, movies and music have been the most successful categories of paid content in recent years.

But most of the content is not premium, and it would have to be advertiser supported. If the advertising option is chosen, then content should be promoted well, and measures should be taken to ensure that the users will be able to access it easily without any glitches. The number of advertisements has to be kept reasonable and relevant to ensure more people access the digital channel. These measures will allow the content producers to enhance the advertising rate of return per user. Most of the YouTube channels are advertiser supported, while some premium content is available on paid channels. YouTube offers advertisers to target specific demographic profiles and geographic locations, offering a lot of value. It also promises not to charge if the ad is skipped by a viewer in between and offers the analytics of the ad for free, making it an attractive proposition.

Content providers can choose to provide both pricing and advertising options simultaneously if access is no longer a problem, and if consumers can be segmented on the basis of willingness to pay. Content producers have to figure out whether their digital users come from the existing traditional advertising or paid channels of distribution and how it affects their overall revenues. As long as the digital platforms help in value migration to the new medium, it is still worth it. If the digital advertising option attracts users from traditionally paid models, it will impact the overall paid revenues negatively. This situation has given rise to popular phrases like "trading analog dollars for digital pennies" by Jeff Zucker, head of NBC Universal, in 2008.

The back catalogues of media content have a lot of value, and that can be unlocked through online distribution. Distribution in the digital format offers many advantages over physical distribution for back catalogues of films, music and re-runs of broadcast shows.

Digital ad spends across the world are growing steadily. Globally, digital ad spends reached 50.1% of total ad spends in 2019, and it was the fastest-growing category in 2019 with a 17.61% increase (emarketer, 2019). Digital ad spends in India are behind North American, European and some Asia Pacific markets. In 2020, digital ad spends at INR 13,683 crores constituted 20% of the total ad spends. In the Indian digital advertising market, social media is the biggest segment, contributing 28% of revenues, followed by paid search at 23%, online video at 22% and display media at 21% respectively (Digital Advertising in India 2020, 6). In the last few years, spends on search and display have been reducing, while spends on social media and video have been increasing. Social media is making money through sponsored posts, promoted tweets, text links and videos. Within the mobile segment, in-app advertisements have a significant share of revenues. With their promises of hyper targeting and immersive advertising, their growth has been good. Revenues of a few digital media companies and divisions are given in Table 8.1.

TABLE 8.1 Revenues of Digital Media Companies

Firm	Revenues 2018–2019 (crores INR)	Profit/Loss 2018–2019 (crores INR)
Google India	4,147	473
Facebook Indian Online Service Pvt Ltd	892	105
Twitter India	56.9	5.8
Times Internet	1526	−102

Source: Compiled from news reports based on ROC data and annual reports.

Digital media revenues in India

Google India reported revenues of INR 4,147 crores in the financial year ending 2019. Google's monopoly over search engine marketing and dominant share in the online video market has helped it to post good revenues across many markets in the world. Daily video views on Facebook and Snapchat have been increasing by millions, giving YouTube good competition. With INR 892 crores, Facebook India posted a 71% rise in revenue in the year 2018–2019.

Times Internet is the biggest digital media company in India. It is a wholly owned subsidiary of The Times Group. Apart from the flagship Indiatimes.com, all the digital editions of the group's newspapers, magazines, TimesMobile, Itimes, BoxTV, Gaana.com. CricBuzz and Coupondunia are part of Times Internet. News aggregator and blogging site Huffington Post India is also co-owned by Times Group. Times Internet posted revenues of INR 1,526 crores and loss of INR 102 crores for the year ending March 31, 2019. Many other traditional media companies including NDTV, HT Media, DB Corp and Dainik Jagran have been reporting increasing revenues from their digital divisions.

Strategies to build market share in the digital space

After the popularisation of TCP/IP, HTTP and HTML technologies in the mid-1990s, many firms in the digital space have been attempting to build proprietary networks to build market share. Whether offline or online, attempts were continuously made to build gateways and ecosystems around them. One of the first such attempts was by Netscape Communications in 1994, when it tried to build a huge market share by giving away their browser Netscape Navigator for free. Their plan was to build a community of users around the free product and to sell server software that complements features of the Netscape browser to website operators. Having established an installed base of millions of users within months, Netscape's proposition for increasing number of commercial organisations wanting to build websites (with their SSL security system) was almost irresistible (Feldman 1997, 115 and 120). Gate-keeping strategies were also built around Internet access provision by dominant ISPs. MCI's Internet Shopping initiative, MarketPlace MCI, intended to leverage the homepage landings, and it was followed with similar attempt by AT&T's Worldnet (Feldman 1997, 121 and 122). Most of these plans to convert Internet into private proprietary networks did not materialise for good reasons. After learning from the initial failures, a new breed of content aggregators and portals came into existence on open access mode.

The evolution of digital landscape is replete with such examples. In 2015, Facebook India tried to increase its market share by offering free Internet access on mobiles by partnering with mobile operator Reliance Communications. This proposal, named "Free Basics," ran into trouble with regulators. According to their plan, Facebook would define the technical guidelines for free basics and reserve the right to reject applications for partnership. It would also keep all the user data. This snowballed into a Net Neutrality debate, and the Telecom Regulatory Authority of India (TRAI) shot down this proposal, citing that it involves offering differential data tariff by telecom operators. These strategies point to the increasing competition in the mobile space. The growing Internet penetration especially on mobile and the increasing ad spends on digital media are clear indicators of the growth in this area. The FICCI-KPMG 2015 report mentions "Second Screen" phenomenon and how it has attracted the attention of content creators and advertisers resulting in "Mobile First" strategies (Shooting for the Stars 2015, 103).

Mobile apps have emerged as a key strategy to increase market share in digital media. All the existing print, radio and television players have developed their custom apps. Most of these apps are downloadable from the App Store and Google Play. Hotstar app, with around 130 million downloads, is from the Star India stable and offers thousands of hours of programming in various languages and various segments including movies, sports and television entertainment. The music app Gaana, with 150 million downloads, and WYNK app from Airtel with 50 million downloads has been a great success in the free music segment. A lot of subscription audio OTT services have been launched in the last few years with national and international players including Spotify, YouTube Music, Amazon Prime Music, Apple Music, Google Play Music, Jio Saavan and Hungama Music. These developments suggest that the battle for market share will be significant in the mobile space, as future of digital media lies there.

Digital rights management

Copyright ownership is the key to exploitation of content by media firms. The idea of ownership in the digital space is complicated, as it breaches geographical boundaries and therefore national laws. Efforts are on to protect copyrights in the digital space through legislations at the national level and through multilateral treaties at the global level. National governments and multilateral agencies have been trying to address the legal and regulatory issues. Apart from ownership issues, some of these laws also try to address aspects like technical standards. The World Intellectual Property Rights Organisation (WIPO) is a specialised agency of the UN. The WIPO Copyright treaty provides copyright protection for databases and prohibits device manufacturers from circumventing technical protection measures such as digital rights management. Many member countries of WIPO adapted these resolutions by enacting national laws beginning with the Digital Millennium Copyright Act 1998 in the United States. Not-for-profit organisations like the International Federation of the Phonographic Industry (IFPI) lobby and fight for implementation of digital music copyrights protection.

Media companies often employ staff to monitor copyrighted content uploaded on popular aggregator sites. Legal content owners routinely submit copyright infringement notifications to sites like YouTube, and they comply by taking them down. Search engine major Google has claimed that it has refined its algorithm to demote websites with many take-down notices for copyright infringement. However, music majors are unhappy with this, and they accuse intermediaries like Google and Bing of directing business to the black market by listing links with pirated content. Digital rights management is still evolving as technological and legal frameworks are still not firmly in place for business models to be built around them with fool proof copyright infringement. DRM also faces much criticism for stifling innovation and competition; more about this will be discussed in Chapter 10 on copyrights.

Key issues for growth of digital media in India

The most important aspect limiting the growth of digital media in India is the lack of infrastructure. Despite Internet penetration in India reaching the 637 million mark in 2019, it is still only around 50% of the Indian population. The average mobile download speed in India at around 12 Mbps and fixed broadband speed at 47 Mbps is significantly lower than the global averages of 35 and 85 Mbps respectively (Ookla Speed Test Global Index 2020). Government initiatives like Digital India are expected to boost the infrastructural requirements of the digital media industry by creating broadband highways and building connectivity to rural areas. Growth of wired connectivity has been slow in the Indian context, and in recent years connectivity growth has been driven by smartphones. As data plans are still expensive, wireless hotspots are being provided for free by government and by some private players.

Apart from infrastructural issues, there are issues related to measurement and analytics, legal framework and policy of taxation. In terms of measuring efficacy, digital media definitely offers better measurability in comparison with other media. However, there are too many data points and too many service providers reducing its value. There are also concerns about non-human traffic affecting the reliability of digital metrics. Taxation is another issue that affects the growth of digital media.

References

#ShootingfortheStars. FICCI-KPMG, Indian Media and Entertainment Industry Report (2015). Retrieved January 6, 2020, from https://assets.kpmg/content/dam/kpmg/pdf/2015/03/FICCI-KPMG_2015.pdf on January 6, 2020

Carroll, G. R., Dobrev, S. D., and Swaminathan, A. (2002). Organizational processes of resource partitioning. *Research in Organizational Behavior, 24*, 1–40.

Digital Advertising in India. (2020). Dentsu Aegis Network. Retrieved June 7, 2021, from https://dentsu.in/uploads/digital_reports/DAN-e4m-Digital-Report-2020-Web-C3.pdf

Doyle, G. (2002). *Understanding Media Economics*. London: Sage Publications.

Economic Impact of the Recorded Music Industry in India (2019, September), Deloitte-Indian Music Industry Report. Retrieved June 7, 2021, from https://www2.deloitte.com/con tent/dam/Deloitte/in/Documents/technology-media-telecommunications/IMI%20 report_singlePage.pdf

Fan, M., Kumar, S., and Whinston, A. B. (2007). Selling or advertising: Strategies for providing digital media online. *Journal of Management Information Systems, 24*(3), 143–166. Retrieved from www.jstor.org/stable/40398899

Feldman, T. (1997). *An Introduction to Digital Media.* New York: Routledge.

Fitzgerald, S. (2019). Over-the-top video services in India: Media imperialism after globalization. *Media Industries, 6*(2), 89–115.

Global Music Report – The Industry in 2019. (2020). IFPI. Retrieved November 14, 2020, from https://www.ifpi.org/wp-content/uploads/2020/07/Global_Music_ Report-the_Industry_in_2019-en.pdf

Newell, J., Pilotta, J. J., and Thomas, J. C. (2008). *Mass Media Displacement and Saturation.* International Journal on Media Management, 10(4), 131–138.

Ookla Speed Test Global Index. (2020). Retrieved November 6, 2020, from www. speedtest.net/global-index

Pavlik, V. J. (2008). *Media in the Digital Age.* New York: Columbia University Press.

Postman, N. (2000). *The Humanism of Media Ecology.* Proceedings of the Media Ecology Association, Vol. 1, 10–16. Retrieved November 17, 2020, from https://www.media-ecology.org/resources/Documents/Proceedings/v1/v1-02-Postman.pdf

Unravelling the Digital Video Consumer. (2019 September). KPMG and Eros Now, 1–45. Retrieved from https://assets.kpmg/content/dam/kpmg/in/pdf/2019/09/ott-digital-video-market-consumer-india.pdf

Zvezdan, V. (2009). Global paradigm shift: Strategic management of new and digital media in new and digital economics. *International Journal on Media Management, 11*(2), 81–90.

9

MEDIA AS CREATIVE INDUSTRIES

In the earlier chapters we talked about the economic properties of media products (i.e., that they are public goods which are non-exclusive and non-rivalrous)
and how these properties shape their production, distribution and consumption.
In this chapter we turn our attention to the broad aspects that are common to all
media industries, so that we can better examine the contexts within which media
products are created and what they mean for media firms and media workers. A
variety of research perspectives have been used to theorise about these industries
(Flew 2011). The political economy perspective, for instance, takes a critical
stance and pays special attention to the power relationships that underpin media
industries and their position in society as well as the role played by these relationships in the creation, distribution and consumption of media products.

A second approach, called the creative industries approach, is a more recent
perspective, and it has its origins in policy interventions in the UK and Australia
in the decade of the 1990s (Flew 2004). Creative industries have been defined
as those that "deal with novel ideas of cultural and social value that are produced by creative people" (Handke and Towse 2013, 1). The creative industries
listed by the British government include media, performing arts, fashion, design
and architecture, among others (Cunningham 2002). According to the International Confederation of Societies of Authors and Composers (CISAC 2015), 11
industries, including advertising, architecture, books, gaming, music, movies,
newspapers and magazines, performing arts, radio, television and visual arts, are
included in creative and cultural industries, and they employ 30 million people worldwide. UNESCO defines creative and cultural industries as industries
"whose principal purpose is production or reproduction, promotion, distribution
or commercialization of goods, services and activities of a cultural, artistic or
heritage-related nature" (cited in CISAC 2015, 11).

DOI: 10.4324/9781003199212-9

In this chapter we examine the research literature on the creative industries for the insights they offer into media industries. This chapter is divided into three sections. The first section examines broad aspects common to creative industries that impact all firms in these industries. The second section presents insights into the nature of work in these industries. The third section examines the opportunities and challenges for media firms given the patterns presented in the previous two sections, and it is followed by the concluding section.

Environment for creative industries

Three aspects—risk, innovation and value (economic, social and cultural)—are considered to be the hallmarks of creative industries (see Handke and Towse 2013; Cunningham 2002; Potts 2013). Of these three aspects, risk is the main element of fundamental economic significance that we see in creative industries (Cunningham 2002). Risk arises from the uncertainty of demand is one of the key properties of creative industries (Caves 2000; Pratt 2013). In Caves's (2003) view:

> "Nobody knows" refers to the fundamental uncertainty that faces the producer of a creative good. All inputs must be incorporated and the good presented to its intended customers before the producer learns their reservation prices. Producers make many decisions that affect the expected quality and appeal of the product, and yet their ability to predict its audience's perception of quality is minimal.
>
> *(Caves 2003, 73)*

As Caves goes on to explain, this uncertainty of demand is common to all the participants in the market and therefore can be seen as a "symmetrical ignorance" or a lack of information. Neither the buyers nor the sellers know if they will want the product until after they have "bought" it and experienced it. This uncertainty arises because each unit of production is unique, as we can see from the example of the film industry (Sedgwick and Pokorny 1998). Many practices seen in these industries are manifestations of the attempts to minimise the impact of risk, including ways of shifting and spreading the risk. At the industry level, we see oligopoly at the distribution stage of the process, with a few large distribution firms as a characteristic feature of creative industries (Pratt 2013). Creative industries typically have two types of firms, large and small, and very few that are mid-sized, leading to a type of a structure that is referred to as the hourglass structure. Therefore, we see an oligopolistic competition structure among the large firms and a perfectly competitive structure among the smaller firms (Flew 2011). At the firm level, we see that Hollywood's film distribution firms have turned to conglomeration, the use of multiple distribution media and even collusion—in markets where they are not prevented from doing so (Christopherson 2008). Additional risk reduction practices, especially in film production firms, include clustering, using networks, co-productions and film financing deals that rely on state subsidies (Morawetz 2007).

In television firms, the "Idol model" is seen as a way to shift the risk to the participants (talent) on reality shows, similar to film festivals which charge entry fees to film makers who submit their films (Christopherson 2008). A further pattern of risk reduction reduces markets for stand-alone products by bundling and integrating products and services and increases consolidation across content production and distribution sectors, also presenting greater economies of scope (van Kranenburg and Ziggers 2013).

Another way that creative industries minimise risk is by using convergence that goes beyond the obvious technological forms. For instance, as Deuze (2009a) points out, convergence in creative industries is seen as the blurring of boundaries between production and consumption. Since it is a well-known fact that consumers demand assurance of quality as well as novelty (Sedgwick and Pokorny 1998), consumers have been drawn into playing a crucial role in shaping how products are created through their active feedback which is solicited at various parts of the production process (Lazzarato 1996). Thus, consumers are co-opted into the production process, blurring the line between production and consumption. We see this taken to its extreme in the development of social media, where content is produced entirely by consumers and distributed through digital media platforms, which use them to generate revenues through advertising, subscription and user data.

Risk is also spread to the workers in the creative industries and has resulted in many accepted labour practices. We will examine these practices in a little more detail in the next section of this chapter.

Innovation is the second hallmark of creative industries. Firms and workers value novelty and actively seek it at all times. These novel ideas are primarily symbolic, as Bilton and Leary (2002) point out:

> "Creative industries" produce "symbolic goods" (ideas, experiences, images) where value is primarily dependent upon the play of symbolic meanings. Their value is dependent upon the end user (viewer, audience, reader, consumer) decoding and finding value within these meanings; the value of "symbolic goods" is therefore dependent on the user's perceptions as much as on the creation of original content, and that value may or may not translate into a financial return.
>
> *(p. 50)*

Innovation is evident in the creation of differentiated products in these industries. No film is exactly same as the previous film. No YouTube video is exactly the same as the previous one. As Caves (2000) observes, differentiated products are one of the key properties of creative industries. Additionally, short product cycles are characteristic features of creative industries (Pratt 2013). Rapidly changing product ranges are seen in creative industries to stimulate repeat and multiple purchases rather than being due to any intrinsic qualities of the products of creative industries, their "ephemerality" is amplified to be seen as adding value (Jeffcutt and Pratt 2002). Innovation and risk go hand in hand in creative industries. Given the high value attached to innovation in creative industries, risk-taking within firms is seen as a crucial necessity. According to Bilton and Leary (2002), "The acceptance of failure, as much as the reward for success, offers an incentive for innovation and risk" (p. 57).

For media professionals such as journalists, the two main motivations to creative work were the opportunities (1) at the personal level to learn new skills and develop competencies such as technology skills which would be assets for future employment, and (2) at the organisational level to develop new practices and processes for the organisation (Malmelin and Virta 2016). At the organisational level, "a collective learning process becomes the heart of productivity, because it is no longer a matter of finding different ways of composing or organizing already existing job functions, but of looking for new ones" (Lazzarato 1996, 135).

The third aspect of creative industries is that they generate value to economies. This is through their dual impact—in a direct way, they contribute to the economy directly through providing employment and attracting consumer spending, and in a more indirect manner, they further promote innovation in the economy by communicating new ideas (Potts 2013). In addition to jobs, the prospect of revenues from international markets are seen as motivating policy decisions in creative industries (Garnham 2005).

Risk, innovation and value are the main factors across creative industries that impact how these industries operate. In the next section, we examine how these factors impact the nature of work in the creative industries.

Issues in managing creativity and creativity as a managed process

An important role in creative industries is played by creative workers, and a key characteristic is that "authorial signature" is valued in these industries (see Cunningham 2002). In this section we examine the literature to identify the aspects that stand out with respect to work in the creative industries. Three aspects, (1) freelance work, (2) urban clustering and (3) the importance of networks, are all well-documented aspects of work in creative industries that apply in a general sense to most media work.

Freelance work is the most important aspect of working in creative industries. When we introduced the topic of risk in the previous section, we noted that firms also spread risk to media workers, and indeed, work in the creative industries is a risky business. Freelance work is the means by which risk is spread from firms to workers (Christopherson 2008). For workers employed by creative firms, risk is, "the necessary corollary, and cost, of their occupation. Indeed, the passionate endorsement of high employment risk is a defining characteristic of the identity of creative workers" (Townley et al. 2009, 951). An important characteristic of freelance work is that not all freelance workers are able to sustain themselves; while some workers at the core manage to find continuous employment, many at the periphery may not have access to work throughout the year (Christopherson 2008). As De Vany (2004) observes, Price's law is supported in film industry work; that is, half the work in an industry is done by the square root of the total participants. In other words, if there are 100 participants in the industry, 10 of them will get to work on 50% of all the projects, while the other 90 participants will have to compete for the remaining 50% of the work. Work that contributes to the informational and cultural content of commodities has been conceptualised as "immaterial labour," which combines intellectual, manual and entrepreneurial skills and can be found in networks and flows rather than within the four walls of a factory, and which is characterised by precariousness, hyperexploitation, mobility, and hierarchy (Lazzarato 1996). In Mumbai's film and television production industries, media workers are contracted to work on individual projects by producers. At the end of the project, workers enter into fresh contracts for new projects as and when such projects become available. Long before the term "gig economy" entered the 21st-century lexicon, freelance work, or project-based employment, has been a key practice in creative industries worldwide and in India.

Freelance work is correlated with fragmented production. Each activity is performed by workers with specific skills, and as Caves (2000) points out, the presence of vertically differentiated skills is one of the key properties of creative industries. However, because creative industries are "collective enterprises" that are embedded in the social and economic realities of a specific location, the relationships within the chain of production must be examined if we want to understand them (Pratt 2008). It is possible that clustering occurs because production activities have become so fragmented (Jeffcutt and Pratt 2002). Thus, creative industries which are simultaneously (1) international (in that their audiences are international) and (2) national (in that they are subject to national governments' policies and regulations—see Flew and McElhinney 2002) also happen to be (3) intensely local with urban clustering at the production level. The well-known real estate adage that focuses on the importance of "location, location, location" is apt for creative industries especially in their production stage. We find plenty of support for Michel Foucault's assertion that "space is fundamental in any form of communal life; space is fundamental in any exercise of power" (Foucault 1984, 252, cited in Flew 2007) and evidence for this view comes especially from research using the cultural and economic geography approach to studying creative industries. While digital media was predicted to usher in the "death of distance," we instead find that media workers are clustered in large cities. Here they benefit from being in touch with the latest developments and access to investment capital through networks bolstered by personal interaction (Pratt 2013).

These urban clusters provide the setting for a crucial element of work in these industries—the networks. Worker's unions provide formal networks and are generally organised by the specialised skills that constitute a craft (see Chitrapu 2017 for a discussion of unions in Mumbai's film and television industries). However, informal networks play an equal if not more important role. Pratt (2008) notes that

> the city is a "high-touch" environment whereby ill-defined and fuzzy knowledges are exchanged—it is a varied informational field within which actors negotiate and filter, and produce, knowledge in a very uncertain wider environment" and these ill-defined aspects can be thought to contribute the most to creative industries.
>
> *(p. 115)*

In addition, "'[g]oing out' becomes part of the job, an opportunity to test out what is popular and a source of market intelligence" (Townley et al. 2009, 948). As Lazzarato (1996) further points out, "It is worth noting that in this kind of working existence it becomes increasingly difficult to distinguish leisure time from work time. In a sense, life becomes inseparable from work" (p. 137).

For instance, for media workers such as those in film production, "trust built on friendship and reputation" is seen as central to belonging to teams and social networks (Kong 2006, 69). Social networks reflect the hierarchies and divisions in society and are seen as excluding women, minorities and younger workers (Christopherson 2008). In special cases such as smaller film markets like Hong Kong, networks in the film production sector are international and include production, financing, cast and crew members from neighbouring industries including those from Taiwan and Beijing (Kong 2006).

In addition to freelance work, urban clustering and networks, there are some conceptualisations of work in creative industries which reveal more nuanced differences, divisions and hierarchies. In this section, we present six of these additional aspects which include (1) the presence of "humdrum inputs," (2) the balance of power between "creatives" and "suits," (3) the importance of intermediaries, (4) the rise of "hybrid" workers and (5) the respatialisation of labour.

When we look closely, the divisions and differences in media labour present themselves in many ways. Media workers in film production, for instance, are divided into above-the-line workers who are paid more and whose "authorial signatures" are valued, which include the directors, actors, music composers, directors of photography and so on; while below-the line workers are those whose inputs are considered replaceable. Below the line, labour is similar to what Caves (2003) refers to as "humdrum inputs—that respond to ordinary economic incentives" (p. 73); this type of labour is especially targeted in leaner budgets (Curtin and Sanson 2016). However, as Jeffcutt and Pratt (2002) argue, "creative" and "non-creative" work in creative industries is interdependent.

A related issue is the balance of power between creative autonomy and corporate functioning. There exists "a delicate and contested balance" between media workers who prefer creative autonomy and the management prerogatives of corporations (Deuze 2009b). This leads to a polarised workforce. "Creatives" and "suits" share an "ambivalent relationship" because creativity is assumed to be located in the individual and not in the processes of the corporation, leading to divisions within the firm (Bilton and Leary 2002).

Given the differences between media workers with different skill sets, the role of intermediaries is important and dynamic in creative industries (Searle and White 2013). Intermediaries such as creative managers combine creative and managerial roles (Flew 2011). These positions typically balance the seemingly conflicting goals of profit for the managerial side and innovative excellence for the creative side. These multifaceted individuals are described as follows: "Creativity brokers do not necessarily possess the talents themselves, but they know how to broker other people's abilities into productive relationships; they also have an eye for the market" (Bilton and Leary 2002, 57).

As in many other industries, creative industries also show downward pressures on pay and upward pressures on hours worked, as firms attempt to reduce labour costs, particularly in sectors where unions are absent (Curtin and Sanson 2016). This has led to trends such as the rise of "hybrid" workers. These are professionals who have multiple skills, such as writer-directors or director-camera-operator-editors, and have learned to work on "shoestring" budgets; such workers are now sought after in American cable television production due to leaner budgets (Christopherson 2008). Media industries are complex environments where multinational companies outsource different parts of the process to smaller independent companies or purchase rights to media products produced by such companies (Deuze 2009b), this has led to the trend called "respatialisation of labour," also known as outsourcing (Curtin and Sanson 2016).

In this section we have taken stock of some key aspects of what it means to work in creative industries. In the next section, we examine what these patterns mean for media firms, in terms of opportunities and challenges.

Opportunities and challenges for media firms

From the previous two sections, we have seen that risk, innovation and value are hallmarks of creative industries and work is of a freelance nature, embedded in urban clusters and heavily dependent on networks. Further, this work shows the presence of "humdrum inputs" and a balance of power between "creatives" and "suits," where intermediaries are important. We have also seen that "hybrid" workers are valued, especially in smaller productions, and respatialisation of labour is a reality. Given the various differences in media work, it becomes evident that media firms need to juggle disparate groups of workers so that their skill sets are complementary in order to innovate in a high-risk business environment. For firms, then, collaboration is therefore identified as a key area. At the industry level, the ability of firms to collaborate with each other has been identified as a valuable competitive advantage, especially their "relational capabilities" in choosing and synchronising with partner firms, and in managing such networks to their mutual advantage (van Kranenburg and Ziggers 2013).

Collaboration and cooperation are seen to be convergent with competition in creative industries and can be thought of as "co-opetition" (Deuze 2009a).

Within a firm, collaboration is seen as key to managing creativity through its impact on managing contexts, connections and balancing dualities such as processes and outcomes; managing individuals and collectives; and permanent and temporary organising (Slavich and Svejenova 2016). Collaboration with a high level of interaction in formal and informal situations that promoted mutual learning and support was seen as inspiring and adding to meaningful work (Malmelin and Virta 2016). Indeed, collaboration is seen to be so important that Lazzarato (1996) argued that it formed the very definition of what it meant to be working, noting that, "Work can thus be defined as the capacity to activate and manage productive cooperation" (p. 134).

Communication is seen as crucial to collaboration. For instance, project management, including communication and information management with respect to goals and the speed of decision making, were identified as key areas of importance because of their impact on multitasking and time pressures, all of which were seen as constraining creative work, especially in journalism (Malmelin and Virta 2016).

Outside firms, collaboration in freelance work is seen in the great reliance on networks in a constant effort to ensure a steady supply of work (Christopherson 2008). While networks are important to creative industries, they are location-specific because of urban clustering (Pratt 2008). Townley et al. (2009) argue that using Bourdieu's (1986) theory of social capital helps us to understand how intellectual capital (creative ideas), social capital (networks) and cultural capital (recognised authority or expertise) contribute to creative industries. It immediately becomes obvious how these networks privilege those with greater social capital and exclude others. Keeping Price's law in mind, some workers are able to access more work than others (De Vany 2004). Further, while changes in technology create a pressure to constantly upgrade skills, we can argue that freelance employment places the burden of reskilling both in terms of time and money on the worker.

In this chapter, we examined creative industries to identify certain broad and nuanced aspects of their functioning. Risk, innovation and value are hallmarks of creative industries. Media workers are primarily freelance workers who rely on networks and are bound by urban clusters. Differences in the value placed on skills and variable access to work govern the work in these industries. Given the fragmented nature of work, collaboration plays an important role at all levels. Above all, creative industries are industries conditioned by risk, and every practice is designed to minimise risk at the firm level, or to cope with risk to the best possible extent at the worker level. To function in these industries, firms and workers need to understand this fundamental quality of creative industries.

References

Bilton, C., and Leary, R. (2002). What can managers do for creativity? Brokering creativity in the creative industries. *International Journal of Cultural Policy, 8*(1), 49–64. https://doi.org/10.1080/10286630290032431

Bourdieu, P. (1986). The forms of capital. In J. Richardson (Ed.), *Handbook of Theory and Research for the Sociology of Education.* Greenwood Press.

Caves, R. E. (2000). *Creative Industries: Contracts between Art and Commerce.* Cambridge, MA: Harvard University Press.

Caves, R. E. (2003). Contracts between art and commerce. *The Journal of Economic Perspectives, 17*(2), 73–84.

Chitrapu, S. (2017). Associations and networks: Inequalities in film and TV production. In A. Athique, V. Parthasarathi, and S. Srinivas (Eds.), *The Indian Media Economy: Market Dynamics and Social Transactions* (Vol. 2, pp. 152–169). Oxford: Oxford University Press.

Christopherson, S. (2008). Beyond the self-expressive creative worker: An industry perspective on entertainment media. *Theory, Culture & Society, 25*(7–8), 73–95.

CISAC. (2015). *Cultural Times: The First Global Map of Cultural and Creative Industries.* Retrieved from https://en.unesco.org/creativity/sites/creativity/files/media_thumb nails/cultural-times_cover.png

Cunningham, S. (2002). From cultural to creative industries: Theory, industry and policy implications. *Quarterly Journal of Media Research and Resources, 102*(1), 54–65.

Curtin, M., and Sanson, K. (2016). *Precarious Creativity: Global Media, Local Labor.* University of California Press.

Deuze, M. (2009a). Convergence culture and media work. In J. Holt and A. Perren (Eds.), *Media Industries: History, Theory, and Method* (pp. 144–156). Wiley-Blackwell.

Deuze, M. (2009b). Media industries, work and life. *European Journal of Communication, 24*(4), 467–480.

De Vany, A. (2004). *Hollywood Economics: How Extreme Uncertainty Shapes the Film Industry.* Abingdon, UK: Routledge.

Flew, T. (2004). Critical communications research in Australia: From radical populism to creative industries. *Javnost: The Public, 11*(3), 31–46.

Flew, T. (2007). *Rethinking Global Media: Creative diversity and media dispersal.* Seoul Symposium on Mobile Communication Mobile Communication and Borderless Society, Seoul, S. Korea.

Flew, T. (2011) Media as creative industries: Conglomeration and globalization as accumulation strategies in an age of digital media. In D. Y. Jin, and D. Winseck (Eds.), *The Political Economies of Media: The Transformation of the Global Media Industries* (pp. 84–100). Bloomsbury Academic.

Flew, T., and McElhinney, S. (2002). Globalization and the Structure of New Media Industries. In L. Lievrouw, and S. Livingstone (Eds.), *Handbook of New Media* (pp. 304–319). SAGE Publications.

Foucault, M. (1984). Space, knowledge and power. *The Foucault Reader, 239*(256).

Garnham, N. (2005). From cultural to creative industries: An analysis of the implications of the "creative industries" approach to arts and media policy making in the United Kingdom. *International Journal of Cultural Policy, 11*(1), 15–29.

Handke, C., & Towse, R. (2013). Introduction. In R. Towse & C. Handke (Eds.), *Handbook on the Digital Creative Economy* (pp. 1-8). Cheltenham, UK: Edward Elgar.

Jeffcutt, P., and Pratt, A. C. (2002). Managing creativity in the cultural industries. *Creativity and Innovation Management, 11*(4), 225–233.

Kong, L. (2006). The sociality of cultural industries: Hong Kong's cultural policy and film industry. *International Journal of Cultural Policy, 11*(1), 61–76.

Lazzarato, M. (1996). Immaterial labour. In P. Virno and M. Hardt (Eds.), *Radical Thought in Italy: A Potential Politics* (pp. 132–146). Choice Publishing Co.; Ltd.

Malmelin, N., and Virta, S. (2016). Managing creativity in change: Motivations and constraints of creative work in a media organisation. *Journalism Practice, 10*(8), 1041–1054.

Morawetz, N. (2007). Finance, policy and industrial dynamics: The rise of co-productions in the film industry. *Industry and Innovation, 14*(4), 421–443. https://doi.org/10.1080/13662710701524072

Potts, J. (2013). Evolutionary perspectives. In R. Towse and C. Handke (Eds.), *Handbook on the Digital Creative Economy* (pp. 26–36). Edward Elgar Publishing. Retrieved from https://EconPapers.repec.org/RePEc:elg:eechap:14906_6

Pratt, A. C. (2008). Creative cities: The cultural industries and the creative class. *Geografiska Annaler: Series B, Human Geography, 90*(2), 107–117.

Pratt, A. C. (2013). Space and place. In R. Towse and C. Handke (Eds.), *Handbook on the Digital Creative Economy* (pp. 37–44). Edward Elgar Publishing. Retrieved from https://EconPapers.repec.org/RePEc:elg:eechap:14906_6

Searle, N., and White, G. (2013). Business models. In C. Handke and R. Towse (Eds.), *Handbook on the Digital Creative Economy* (pp. 45–56). Edward Elgar Publishing. Retrieved from https://EconPapers.repec.org/RePEc:elg:eechap:14906_6

Sedgwick, J., and Pokorny, M. (1998). The risk environment of film making: Warner Bros in the inter-war years. *Explorations in Economic History, 35*(2), 196–220.

Slavich, B., and Svejenova, S. (2016). Managing creativity: A critical examination, synthesis, and new frontiers. *European Management Review, 13*(4), 237–250.

Townley, B., Beech, N., and McKinlay, A. (2009). Managing in the creative industries: Managing the motley crew. *Human Relations, 62*(7), 939–962.

van Kranenburg, H., and Ziggers, G. W. (2013). Dynamic competition and ambidexterity. In R. Towse and C. Handke (Eds.), *Handbook on the Digital Creative Economy* (pp. 57–66). Edward Elgar Publishing. Retrieved from https://EconPapers.repec.org/RePEc:elg:eechap:14906_6

10

COPYRIGHTS AND MEDIA BUSINESS

Understanding copyrights

Copyright can be defined as a creator's exclusive right to reproduce, publish, adopt, translate, give on hire, assign, sell or even relinquish rights of the original work of authorship. The "original work" can be a literary, dramatic or musical work, film, TV or radio broadcast, computer programme, blog or a range of other creative works. Copyrights in India are governed by Indian Copyrights Act 1957. It was amended from time to time to keep up with technological changes and multilateral trade agreements. The amendments in 1994, 1999 and 2012 are significant.

Across the world, all copyright acts insist on "expression" for being eligible for copyright protection. Any original expression is eligible for copyright protection as soon as it is fixed in a tangible form. For example, a graphic created in Photoshop is protected as soon as the file is saved on the system. However, only expressions are eligible for copyrights, not ideas. The principle that copyright protects the expression of ideas but does not protect the ideas themselves is known as the "idea/expression distinction" in copyright jurisprudence. The doctrine was developed in the United States and is accepted globally as a central axiom in copyright law.

The idea/expression distinction that enables copyright protection in jurisprudence was tested in the Indian context with the case *R. G. Anand v. Delux Films*. Anand filed an infringement case against the makers of the film *New Delhi* (1956), accusing them of plagiarising his play *Hum Hindustani* (1953). The central theme and the plot structure of the two works were similar and Mohan Sehgal, owner of Delux Films, had a discussion with the playwright in a meeting. Mr. Sehgal on his part claimed that he always wanted to make a film on this theme and submitted that he informed the playwright that the play may be

DOI: 10.4324/9781003199212-10

good for the stage but not for a full-length commercial film. The Supreme Court of India laid down tests and principles to determine copyright infringement in this case. Firstly, there can be no copyright in ideas, so similarity of the theme cannot be an infringement; secondly, infringement can be established only by examining the form, manner and arrangement of expression of an idea in the "imitated work" in comparison with the copyrighted work. The court ruled that the film cannot be regarded as a substantial copy of the play, observing, "but for the central idea (not protected by copyright), from scene to scene, situation to situation, in climax to anti-climax, pathos, in texture and treatment and purport and presentation, the picture is materially different from the play" (Reddy and Chandrasekharan 2017, 158–162). In the case of *Barbara Taylor Bradford v. Sahara Media Entertainment Ltd.*, the plaintiff charged that the television serial *Karishma—The Miracle of Destiny* is a copy of her novel *A Woman of Substance*. The petitioners based their claim on an interview by the show producer to a journalist, wherein he claimed it took the "rags to riches" theme from the book. Going by earlier precedents, the court ruled that there could be no copyright in theme and observed that infringement can be established only by examining the form, manner and arrangement of the expression.

Understanding copyright mechanisms requires familiarity with a set of concepts including copyright registry, copyright term, copyright infringement, fair use, public domain, and copyright societies. They will be discussed in detail with relevant case studies in the following pages.

Copyright registry

Even though copyright law affords automatic copyright protection as in the case of the Photoshop file discussed earlier in the chapter, it also makes it amply clear that it is desirable to register the works with the copyright office. Registered works go through verification before being included in the Register of Copyrights. Registered copyright works have better legal standing in the case of copyright infringement. In the case of *B.K. Dani v. State of M.P* (2004), the ruling contended that in the absence of copyright registration, copyright infringement cannot be claimed. It has also become customary to give a copyright notice—to put the world on notice that they are dealing with a copyrighted work. A typical copyright notice looks like this:

In India, Copyright Act 1957 made provisions for creation of the Copyright Office and Copyright Board. The Registrar of Copyright Office administers the registration process, while the Chairman of Copyright Board, a quasi-judicial body, adjudicates disputes arising out of copyright administration (The Indian Copyright Act 1957, 6–7). In 2017, the government, with an intention to reduce the number of tribunals, merged the Copyright Board with the Intellectual Property

Appellate Board, another tribunal created under Trade Marks Act 1999. All the cases pending with the Copyright Board were transferred to the new Board.

Copyright term

Copyright term refers to the duration or period in which the copyright subsists before it enters the public domain. During this period, the lawful owner enjoys the exclusive rights. After the exclusive rights expire on completion of the copyright term, they become part of the public domain. The public domain also consists of works that were created before the Copyright Acts came into existence. The early publishers and film industries benefitted extensively by drawing from the public domain. According to Indian Copyright Act, the term of copyright varies with the type of work. Some examples are given here.

Term of copyright in published literary, dramatic, musical and artistic works subsist within the lifetime of the author and until 60 years from the beginning of the calendar year next following the year in which the author dies. Whereas, in anonymous and pseudonymous works, term of copyright shall subsist for 60 years from the beginning of the next calendar year. If the identity of the author is disclosed before the expiry of the said period, copyright shall subsist until 60 years from the beginning of the calendar year next following the year in which the author dies.

Term of copyright in cinematograph films and sound recording subsist until 60 years from the beginning of the calendar year next following the year in which they are published. Term of copyright in a broadcast shall subsist until 25 years from the beginning of the calendar year next following the year in which the broadcast is made (The Indian Copyright Act 1957, 13–14).

Longer copyright terms have been very controversial as they are seen as favouring corporates. In the United States, Disney is charged with lobbying extension of copyright terms whenever its Mickey Mouse is set to enter the public domain. Disney, which has benefited immensely in its early stages by drawing on works in the public domain, including Cinderella, has been charged with unwillingness to let go of its works into the public domain. Mickey Mouse is once again set to enter the public domain in 2023 and may kick-start a fresh round of debate around extension of copyrights. In India, Copyright Amendment Act 2010 extended the copyright term of cinematograph film to 70 years from 60 by allowing the principal film director as joint author along with the producer. Director's rights subsist for 70 years while the producers subsist for 60. This is seen a result of lobbying work by Yash Raj Films.

Copyright infringement

Copyright in a work shall be deemed to be infringed when someone unauthorisedly uses works protected under copyright law. If unauthorised reproduction, distribution, adaptation, performance, display or commercial exploitation happens, the original lawful owner of the copyright can issue take-down notices, negotiate a settlement or file a lawsuit for infringement and damages. Copyright laws have provisions to deal with infringement both under civil and criminal law depending on the nature of the infringement.

One of the important issues that arose with emergence of digital media economy is the issue of intermediary liability. To what extent are intermediaries such as ISPs, search engines and digital platforms responsible for copyright infringement? Safe harbour provisions for intermediaries have been provided under IT Act 2000 and Copyright Amendment Act 2012 (Sethia 2017, 401). The case, *Super Cassette Industries v. Myspace Inc.* in 2016, laid down principles for intermediary rights and responsibilities. By ruling that Myspace is an "intermediary" and therefore cannot be held for primary infringement for the acts committed by a third party on their platform, the court affirmed the safe harbour provisions. It is only when the platforms do not respond to the take-down notices for infringing content, the digital safe harbour provisions get denied. More recently, the *Swami Ramdev v. Facebook* judgement in 2019 laid down principles regarding responsibilities of intermediaries and the jurisdiction of Indian courts. The book, titled *Godman to Tycoon—the Untold Story of Baba Ramdev*, was restrained from being published by the Delhi High Court for containing defamatory material against Baba Ramdev. However, many videos of summaries of the book were circulating online. Baba Ramdev and Patanjali Ayurveda went to court asking for a global take-down order to be issued to remove the content from Google, Facebook, YouTube, Twitter and other unidentified intermediaries. The court ruled that content uploaded from India can be ordered to be taken down globally. For content uploaded from outside India, the court ordered that platforms should use appropriate geo-blocking measures to ensure the content is not available in India. In this case, the court tried to strike a balance between free speech and individual privacy in its order.

Fair use in copyright law

Fair use is an exemption from copyright infringement claim for uses that are fair. Countries across the world have made legal provisions for fair use. It also acts as a check on the unlimited power "to use," of the supposed creators on their work. Despite the legal stipulation, it remains a highly contentious provision within copyright law.

Section 52 of Copyright Act 1957 lists that "certain acts not be infringement of copyright" (The Indian Copyright Act 1957, 32–37). Some of them include:

- A fair dealing with a literary, dramatic, musical or artistic work for the purpose of reporting current events in a newspaper or magazine or by broadcast or in a cinematograph film or by means of photographs.
- The reproduction of a literary, dramatic, musical or artistic work for the purpose of a judicial proceeding.
- The reproduction or publication of a literary, dramatic, musical or artistic work in any work prepared by the secretariat of a legislature or, where the

legislature consists of two houses, by the secretariat of either house of the legislature, exclusively for the use of the members of that legislature.

- The reading or recitation in public of any reasonable extract from a published literary or dramatic work.
- To make back-up copies purely as a temporary protection against loss, destruction or damage in order only to utilise the computer programme for the purpose for which it was supplied.

The fair use exemptions under Section 52 of the Indian Copyright were tested in the Delhi University Photocopy case. A few reputed academic publishers sued a photocopy shop and the University of Delhi for copyright infringement. The case is important because it reveals the thin line that exists between fair dealing and infringement. The publishers alleged that extracts from their copyrighted works were photocopied into course packs and sold by the photocopy shop, which amounts to infringement. The defendants pleaded that their usage has to be considered as "fair use" in this case for the purpose of instruction. The division bench of Delhi High Court did not agree with the arguments of the plaintiffs and ruled that photocopies which are made a part of students' reading material, even without the permission of the copyright holder, are non-infringing as long as it is "in the course of instruction." The judgement was welcomed by many student groups and teachers working for equitable access to education and knowledge. However, some argue that this ruling has interpreted "academic fair dealing exception" more liberally and extended it to people who are only remotely academic and ignored the extent of infringement and commercial exploitation involved (Gosh 2016, 1). Later, the publishers withdrew the suit and expressed that they were not interested in pursuing this matter in higher courts.

Around the same time, a copyright society by the name Indian Reprographic Rights Organisation (IRRO) was started on behalf of publishers to licence photocopying and collect royalties from universities and commercial photocopying shops. Slowly, they seem to be making progress, as some universities and colleges have taken IRRO licences, which as of now has a reasonably priced tariff scheme.

Copyright societies

Monitoring use of copyrights and monetising them is a very expensive affair and is not economically viable for most of the copyright owners. Hence, they entrust this job to collectives specialising in copyright administration. Creative individuals and outfits which are supposed to produce intellectual property cannot spend time and resources on copyright administration, so they depend on specialised collectives for this job. As per copyright law, the societies should have open membership and should be non-discriminatory. In most of the countries, the law places pricing limits for licence fees and protects equitable distribution of collected fees among the rights holders. In India, Copyright Rules 2013 mandate copyright societies to publish tariff schemes, maintain a Register of Royalties with details of royalties collected and keep a Disbursement Register with the details of disbursements made to the rights holders.

The Indian Copyright Act 1957 has made provisions for formation of copyright societies to administer copyrights under section 33. For instance, in the case of the music industry in India, PPL and Indian Performing Rights Society (IPRS) are two big copyright societies. Blanket licences are very popular for music among radio broadcasters, wherein they licence the whole repertoire for unlimited use for specific time periods. Indian Reprographic Rights Organisation (IRRO) is one of the youngest copyright societies in India, created in 2000, to issue reprographic licences (printing, photocopying, scanning etc.) on behalf of publishers.

There have been debates on the ideal number of societies required for efficient and democratic functioning of the markets. If a single copyright society performs this activity, it might be economically efficient for a given market. However, it might also lead to monopoly situations and abuse of monopoly power. Too many societies in a given market will also make it inefficient. A reasonable number of societies competing with each other, probably will increase overall market efficiency if the market they are serving is big. These copyright societies also enter into reciprocal arrangements with other such societies in other countries. Their reach and economic efficiency make them the de facto choice for the copyright owners in a given market. Collective licencing administration has almost become inevitable and not a choice. In most countries, the copyright laws lay down strict rules for the functioning of copyright societies, thereby restricting them from becoming monopolies. The administrative costs should be less for efficient collectives; if the costs are high, the copyright owners may leave the collective for a competitor or do it themselves.

A brief history of copyright law

The first Copyright Act was passed by Britain in 1710. As per this Act, the term of copyright was for a period of 14 years, renewable for another 14 years. The United States modelled its Copyright Act 1790 on the lines of the British Act. This act protected only the rights of American authors, denying international copyright protection. This policy opened doors for official piracy in America. Most of the British works were printed and sold by American publishers without paying any royalty. This changed only in 1891, when the US Congress passed the International Copyright Act 1891, affording protection to foreign copyright holders from select nations.

As long as it suited American interests and as long as America was a cultural importer, they were ideologically for public utility; and once they became cultural exporters, their ideologies and interests started to converge in protecting author's rights. The American content industry's concerns became important, and they were dovetailed into the economic policies related to culture. With this, the lenient attitude towards piracy disappeared, and aggressive implementation of copyright protection became more important.

The Berne Convention, Universal Copyright Convention did not have proper enforcement mechanisms built into them when violations took place in foreign territories. The Trade Related Intellectual Property Rights (TRIPS) agreement 1994 under the WTO framework provided legal basis for copyright protection in foreign countries. All member countries were expected to make changes in their domestic copyright laws to comply with this agreement. TRIPS also made possible imposition of trade sanctions against nations not acting on copyright violations. Developed countries such as the United States, whose economy gains a lot from intellectual property, have developed unilateral enforcement mechanisms to protect their interests (Desai 2005, 263). By the late 20th century, the United States started unilaterally implementing its "Special 301" regulations of the US Trade Act to enforce protection of American intellectual property rights in foreign countries. The Special 301 provision under the US Trade Act 1988 enables it to initiate investigations and to evaluate the level of intellectual property protections offered by other states. These investigation results might lead to placing a nation on watch list, impositions of sectoral and cross-sectoral sanctions or even withdrawal of trade privileges. Multilateral bodies like WIPO and WTO are currently at the forefront in enforcing copyrights globally.

Copyright law in India

The Indian Copyright Act 1914 was an application and adaptation of British Copyright Act 1911, for British India. The Act "extend[ed] to the whole of British India including British Baluchistan, the district of Angul and the Sonthal Parganas" (The Indian Copyright Act 1914, 7). This Act was not applicable in the numerous self-governing dominions unless adapted by the legislature of that dominion. According to Upendra Baxi, a legal scholar, princely states like Hyderabad, the Portuguese and the French enclaves in India, and even the East India Company, had copyright systems in some form. He argues that without considering them, and instead starting the history of copyright law in India with the Act of 1914 would lead to misreading the contexts (Baxi 1986, 2–3). This complicated status led to issues related to copyright enforcement in British India. One of the early concerns of film piracy in India was addressed by the report of the Cinematograph Committee 1927–1928. The committee looked into the complaints of exhibitors that their exclusive rights for distributing imported films was infringed through circulation of pirated copies by other distributors. The committee felt that the existing legal remedies were not adequate and suggested registration of exclusive rights of distribution with the Central Cinema Bureau (which the committee recommended), which after examining the documents would issue certificate for exhibition (Report of the Indian Cinematograph Committee 1927–1928, 85).

After India became independent, the Indian constitution recognised laws enacted by British India for administrative convenience. This included the Indian Copyright Act 1914. This also meant that India had to adhere to multilateral agreements such as Berne Convention which British India was part of. The Berne Convention laid down criteria required to be adhered to by the member countries in their domestic copyright law, such as the minimum copyright term and the recognition of foreign copyrights (Reddy and Chandrasekharan 2017, 117).

As revenues from creative industries started increasing, the importance of copyright law became more evident. For instance, the Indian music market grew at a rapid pace after the introduction of cassette technology in the late 1970s and early 1980s. However, the easy possibilities of copying music on tape made 90% of music market illegal. Music piracy, although illegal, was not a punishable offence under the original act. It was only through the 1994 amendment that music piracy was made a punishable offence with fines and imprisonment (Booth 2015, 271). Music companies with legal rights were almost bankrupt in the 1980s. Indian Phonographic Industry (IPI), later renamed Indian Music Industry (IMI), has been complaining that some of the fair use provisions have been misused to infringe copyrights and indulge in commercial exploitation with version recordings and remixes.

The music industry also had other issues, such as who has the copyright over a piece of composed music. In the case of the Indian film industry, the lyricists, composers and singers felt side-lined by film producers. The film producers engaged the artists on a contractual basis and retained the rights over the music, assigned them to music labels and earned royalties. In the case, *Indian Performing Rights Society v. Eastern Indian Motion Pictures Ltd.* (1977), IPRS, a copyright society on behalf of artists, claimed that it was entitled to royalties on music incorporated in cinematograph films, if it was broadcast over radio. As a copyright society working on behalf of its assignees, it came out with a tariff scheme for radio stations. The association of film producers contested it by claiming that they were the absolute owners of the copyright and the lyricists and composers had no right over the work, as they lost their right by entering into a contract to provide the service for a fee. The court ruling was decisively in favour of the film producers. The judgement stated that unless there was an agreement to the contrary, film producers were the absolute owners of copyright if they have contracted the services for a fee and also had rights of assignment over future uses. The Copyright Amendment Act 2012 reversed this by incorporating provisions, which retained the rights of the lyricists and composers as first authors despite its incorporation in a cinematograph film. This enabled the lyricists, composers and singers, or copyright societies on their behalf, to claim royalties.

Copyright debates

The debates on copyrights evoke strong responses. On one side are copyright minimalists, and on the other copyright maximalists. Most of the activists acting on behalf of general public interest prefer the minimal approach to the institution of copyrights. Whereas, the maximalists, generally the commercial copyright owners and their agents, prefer an expansionist approach. These forces counter each other, and this tension helps in evolving a pragmatic approach to copyrights. A good copyright policy has to balance the market-oriented concerns and the public interest concerns in an effective way.

In the mid-20th century Europeans increasingly regarded intellectual property as founded on natural rights in two ways: as a form of quasi-conventional property based on Lockean ownership via labour but also as an emanation of the author's personality (Baldwin 2014, 384). Equating information, images, sound and literature to property and assigning them rights on par was always contested. The access rights of people to creative works had to be balanced along with the authorial rights. However, starting from the Berne Convention in 1928, commercial interests have largely managed to get acceptance to creative works as natural rights through strong copyright protection laws (Baldwin 2014, 384).

More recently, development of the digital markets led to new changes in the copyright laws. The digital platforms enabled wider access to markets but also posed threats by increasing online unauthorised use of copyrighted products. Copyrights holders started using digital rights management technologies such as watermarks and encryption. However, they are not foolproof and are prone to circumvention. The World Intellectual Property Organisation (WIPO) advocates for inclusion of legal remedies against circumvention of digital rights management technologies and protection of digital rights management information in domestic laws. Copyright Amendment 2012 introduced digital rights management provisions in Indian law. It harmonises Indian law with international law, in a context where India has not ratified WIPO Internet Treaties. The US adoption of WIPO Digital Rights Management provisions happened through the controversial Digital Millennium Copyrights Act. The DRM provisions by extending the copyright law to copyright protection mechanisms are accused of stretching the traditional boundaries of copyright law and for creating a para-copyright regime (Scaria 2012, 465). Critics point out that due economic analysis and social welfare were not adequately considered before enacting these amendments.

There is a need to strike a balance between the minimalist and maximalist approaches to copyright law. According to Balganseh, Gandhi's copyright pragmatism allowed him to engage with it reluctantly and deploy it strategically, while rejecting it personally. For instance, he retained his first right to translate his newspaper articles, while relinquishing the right once they were translated. He bequeathed copyrights in his works to Navjivan Trust and not to his children, as the Copyright Act permits. Gandhi's pragmatism allowed him to acknowledge the importance of copyright as a mechanism for attribution, while separating copyright's market-based aspects from its attributive ones. As a way of thinking, copyright pragmatism allows copyright scholars, lawyers and activists to adopt a midway position between the extremes of copyright nihilism, or minimalism, and copyright expansionism, or maximalism—the dominant positions in today's "copyright wars" (1711).

Arguments for copyrights

Copyrights enabled authors to become independent from the bondage and servility of the patronage system, which was prominent in medieval times. Authors in the 19th and 20th centuries were able to exercise artistic independence as they could depend on revenues from the markets. It allowed authors to have fair returns for their creative labour and allowed them to have a dignified livelihood. Over two centuries, copyright regimes have incentivised creativity, protected author's rights and ensured competitive advantage for creative individuals and firms. Implicit in incentivising production of expression through copyright protection is the idea that it contributes to social welfare and the progress of society.

Creative industries employ a lot of people and contribute significantly to the GDP of nations. Protecting the economy of creative industries in a market rife with piracy is possible only through enforcing copyright exclusively in favour of copyright holders. This means the authorial rights cannot be diluted from an economic standpoint. Supporters argue that lack of strong and enforceable copyright laws inhibit development of economically functional creative industries (Barblan 2013). They argue that copyright mechanisms have a larger role in supporting a free market economy for creative works, and not just in protecting the exclusive rights of authors. Copyright enthusiasts argue that efficient free markets cannot occur without strong underlying property rights and weakening copyright mechanisms will only hamper growth of creative industries.

Arguments against copyrights

Copyright regimes have been facing criticism for being over-inclusive, generating barriers to creativity, ever greening by corporates, excluding low-paying consumers and creating segment monopolies. Highly priced copyright products pose a major access and cost challenge for the low-income groups. Copyrights are provided for producing and disseminating creative works. When it does not serve the purpose, the right of the copyright holder is not justified. Critics argue that ownership cannot be the sole criterion for deciding the use. It is necessary to have checks on the unlimited legal power that is derived by the creators from holding the copyright. Shorter copyright terms and extensive fair use provisions are being advocated as solutions to the ills of copyright regimes.

Apart from the consumers, absolute copyright ownerships can cause problems to other players in the market. Sometimes dominant firms abuse the advantage acquired through copyright ownership by refusing to licence, affecting firms down the line and resulting in restricted access to end consumers. This comes at the intersection of competition law and copyright law, which work for safeguarding equitable market access and innovation respectively. The remedy available for abusive refusal to licence is the imposition of compulsory licencing on IPR holders (Khanna 2019, 49). In the Indian context, the case *HT Media v. T-Series* would be useful in understanding how IPR-related dominance affects firms down the line. HT Media, which runs FM radio stations under the brand name "Fever FM," filed a case before the Competition Commission of India (CCI) against T-Series for abusing its market dominance by charging royalties in excess of those suggested by the Copyright Board. CCI ruled that it found T-Series to be in a dominant position in the relevant market, and it violated competition norms by imposing unfair conditions on FM radio stations. It further ruled ordering T-Series to "cease and desist" from anti-competitive practices and modify the unfair conditions imposed on FM stations.

This mercantile approach to culture has been a matter of concern for copyright critics. The idea of autonomous authorship wherein authors create ex nihilo is being contested. They do not see creative works as creations of solitary romantic genius, but as socially determined and collective. The commons angle is acknowledged in this formulation. The fundamental reliance of copyrights on artificial scarcity, market-based distribution and profit-driven inducement of expressing creativity have been fundamental issues for copyright critics. They look at the spirit of commons as an antidote to these problems.

Open access movements

Critics have charged copyright systems with working with capitalist logics by enabling a commodification process and disabling commons and community. To challenge the increasingly pervasive and hegemonic logics of capital in the digital spaces and bring back the spirit of commons, many initiatives have been launched in the last three decades. Going by different nomenclatures—Digital Commons, Open Access, and Copyleft—they intend to develop alternative practices that foster the spirit of sharing, reciprocity and community, besides countering the commodification process enabled by the copyright regimes. The digital commons is a new frontier for struggles over commodification. It is a space that enables counter-commodification—not just on a personal but on a global level. It demonstrates how creative work can flourish without the chains of intellectual property regulations (Wittel 2013, 329).

One of the most durable arguments for Open Access (OA) is that knowledge is and ought to be a public good. Even copyright laws privatise expression of ideas, while leaving the ideas themselves unprivatised, unregulated and public. It means the texts are not public goods, even if the knowledge they contain remains a public good. Hence, to remove impediments to knowledge-sharing, the job isn't to make knowledge a public good, which is already done. The job is to make texts into public goods as well (Suber 2016, 3–4). OA efforts in the domain of education and research have been working with this objective. With low replication costs, the possibility of making texts into public goods is much higher in the digital form. OA removes price barriers and permission barriers, making texts non-rivalrous and non-excludable. Many authors have been supporting OA initiatives by making their texts available in OA journals.

Universities for their part have been hosting OA repositories. Many non-OA journals also allow their authors to deposit a preprint or post-print version in OA repositories. Some grant-making bodies are mandating their grantees to submit their research output to OA journals and repositories making them more mainstream. In their efforts to create discoverable and usable creative commons, the global community of commons has created enormous public archival platforms. Activists and civil society groups have been creating digital archives by recording memories and oral histories with an intention to deepen democratic values and increase public engagement. These platforms could be mined by scholars from social sciences, humanities and digital and technology studies to understand the myriad phenomena of interest to their respective disciplines.

A system of Public Copyright Licences has been developed to promote open access not just in academics but also in other spheres of creative activities. Creative Commons licences issued by a US-based non-profit body are popular among authors and artists, especially the Creative Commons BY licence which expects nothing more than attribution for the work used. Public licences in the software domain include the popular GNU General Public license for free and open-source software. These licences allow users and developers to use, share and modify the software. However, these Copyleft licences expect the derivative works to be distributed under the same or similar licence terms. Apart from these, a multitude of commons have proliferated in the last few decades, sometimes with public funding.

In this chapter we examined some important concepts related to copyrights and media business. Each of these concepts, including the idea/expression distinction, copyright registry, copyright term, copyright infringement, fair use and copyright societies, were discussed with relevant case studies. The chapter also briefly dealt with the history of copyright law globally and in India besides addressing debates and movements around copyrights.

Conclusion

Understanding the principles of media economics is fundamental to building a working knowledge of media industries, media policies and emerging issues in media industries such as the gig economy and labour networks. Media industries around the world are moving towards greater consolidation. Media policies are being designed to ensure, among other things, an even playing field while supporting innovation, and media workers are scrambling to keep pace with changing technology and professional cultures. While newer forms of technology and media consumption vie for our attention, more established forms undergo changes to stay profitable and relevant. Powerful economic forces propel changes in all these areas, and not only media economics researchers, but students, practitioners and researchers belonging to critical and other perspectives who are interested in the media can benefit from familiarising themselves with how these forces operate and their far-reaching impacts on content, policies and audiences.

References

Baldwin, P. (2014). Conclusion: Reclaiming the spirit of copyright. In *The Copyright Wars: Three Centuries of Trans-Atlantic Battle* (pp. 383–410). Princeton and Oxford: Princeton University Press. Retrieved from www.jstor.org/stable/j.ctt6wq0z2.12

Barblan, M. (2013). Copyright is still essential to a free market in creative works. *Center for Copyright Protection of Intellectual Property*. Retrieved November 13, 2002, from https://cpip.gmu.edu/2013/11/14/copyright-is-still-essential-to-a-free-market-in-creative-works/

Baxi, U. (1986). Copyright law and justice in India. *Journal of the Indian Law Institute, 28*(4), 497–540.

Booth, G. (2015, Spring/Summer). Copyright law and the changing economic value of popular music in India. *Ethnomusicology, 59*(2), 262–287.

Desai, R. (2005, Spring). Copyright infringement in the Indian film industry. *Vanderbilt Journal of Entertainment Law & Practice. 7*, 259–263.

Gosh, E. (2016). Fundamental errors in fundamental places: A case for setting aside the Delhi university photocopying judgement. *NUJS Law Review, 9*(1).

The Indian Copyright Act, 1914. Retrieved March 21, 2020, from www.wipo.int/edocs/lexdocs/laws/en/in/in121en.pdf

The Indian Copyright Act, 1957. Retrieved March 21, 2020 from www.wipo.int/edocs/lexdocs/laws/en/in/in107en.pdf

Khanna, P. (2019). Abuse of dominant position by refusing to issue copyright licenses. *Christ University Law Journal, 8*(2), 45–61.

Reddy, P. T., and Chandrasekharan, S. (2017). *Create, Copy, Disrupt: India's Intellectual Property Dilemmas.* New Delhi, India: Oxford University Press.

Report of the Indian Cinematograph Committee 1927–1928. Retrieved September 4, 2020, from https://ia802608.us.archive.org/34/items/reportoftheindia030105mbp/reportoftheindia030105mbp.pdf

Scaria, A. G. (2012, September). Does India need digital rights management provisions or better digital management strategies. *Journal of Intellectual Property Rights, 17*, 463–477.

Sethia, A. (2017). The troubled waters of copyright safe harbours in India. *Journal of Intellectual Property Law & Practice, 12*(5), 398–407.

Suber, P. (2016). *Knowledge Unbound: Selected Writings on Open Access, 2002–2011.* Cambridge, MA: MIT Press. Retrieved from http://nrs.harvard.edu/urn-3:HUL.InstRepos:2624607

Wittel, A. (2013). Counter-commodification: The economy of contribution in the digital commons. *Culture and Organization, 19*(4), 314–331. doi:10.1080/14759551.2013.827422

INDEX

Printed in the United States
by Baker & Taylor Publisher Services